COMMON SENSE INVESTING IN REAL ESTATE

ADVANCED CONCEPTS OF
COMMON SENSE INVESTING IN REAL ESTATE

*Learn the Smartest, Safest and
Most Profitable Ways of Making Money
In Residential Real Estate*

LARRY and CONNIE GARRETT

Sunrise Publishing, LLC

All rights reserved. No part of this book may be reproduced in any form or by any electronic or mechanical means including information storage and retrieval systems—except in the case of brief quotations embodied in critical articles or reviews—without permission in writing from its publisher, Sunrise Publishing LLC. Purchasers of the book are granted license to use the forms contained herein for their own personal use. No claim of copyright is made to any government form reproduced herein. All brand names and product names used in this book are trademarks, registered trademarks, or trade names of the respective holders.

Published by:
Sunrise Publishing LLC
2334 W Quail Track Drive
Phoenix, AZ 85085
602-494-4187

Cover and book design: Jane Perini
Layout and production: Atara Heiss
Thunder Mountain Design & Communications, Sedona, AZ

This publication is designed to provide accurate and authoritative information in regard to the subject matter covered. It is sold with the understanding that the publisher is not engaged in rendering legal, accounting, or other professional service. If legal advice or other expert assistance is required, the services of a competent professional person should be sought.

This product is not a substitute for legal advice. Consult your attorney or CPA for legal and/or accounting advise.

ISBN: 978-0-6152-4418-1
© 2008 by Larry and Connie Garrett

CONTENTS

Acknowledgments 9

A Note to Readers 11

CHAPTER ONE: THE EIGHT PILLARS 13

Pillar 1:   You should be Excited 19

Pillar 2:   You need to be able to see Long Term Potential 20

Pillar 3:   The 20/20/60 Rule; Buy Smart, Sell High, Manage Well ... 21

Pillar 4:   Stay Close to Centers of Employment 21

Pillar 5:   Buy Into Growth Areas 22

Pillar 6:   The Yield Curve is the Best Leading Indicator 23

Pillar 7:   Location, Location, & Location 24

Pillar 8:   Timing is Extremely Important 25

CHAPTER TWO: UNDERSTANDING INTEREST RATES 29

Insight 1:   Do Not Fight the Feds 31

Insight 2:   As Interest Rates Go Up, Property Values Decline 32

Insight 3:   As Interest Rates Go Up, Rents Increase 36

Insight 4:   The Federal Reserve 37

Insight 5:   The Yield Curve, Better Than a Crystal Ball 45

Insight 6:   The Tilt-a-Whirl Ride 51

CHAPTER THREE: IMPORTANT CONCEPTS 55

Insight 7:   Newer Properties Appreciate Faster 57

Insight 8:   You Must Have Adequate Reserves 58

Insight 9:   Two Big Common Mistakes that Investors Make 62

Insight 10: If Something Can Go Wrong, It Probably Will 63

Insight 11: Fool's Gold 65

Insight 12: Real Gold 66

Insight 13: Make Money in a Slow Market 70

Insight 14: Buy into a Soft Market 72

Insight 15: Check Out Recent Comparables 76

Insight 16: Fools Rush in Where Angels Fear to Tread 79

CHAPTER FOUR: THE MAGIC OF THE INTERNET 83

Insight 17: Utilizing the Internet with Real Estate Investments 85

CHAPTER FIVE: BUYERS PREPARATION 91

Insight 18: Buying a House Can be Confusing 93

Insight 19: Consumer Debt Versus Investment Debt 96

Insight 20: Understand Your Mortgage Options 102

Insight 21: There is No Such Thing as "No Costs Mortgage" 109

Insight 22: Use a Professional Full Time REALTOR® and Loan Officer 112

Insight 23: Your First Purchase should be Owner Occupied 117

Insight 24: Real Estate should be a Long Term Investment 119

Insight 25: Hold On For the Long Haul 122

CHAPTER SIX: ADDITIONAL INTUITIVE CONCEPTS 127

Insight 26: The Pros and Cons of Negative Cash Flow 129

Insight 27: A Reverse Mortgage can be a Retirees Financial Salvation 133

Insight 28: You are Buying to Sell 135

Insight 29: Outlying Areas Get Hit the Hardest 137

Insight 30: Condos First to Go Down 139

Insight 31: Think About What You're Buying 140

Insight 32: High Demand Areas 141

Insight 33: Schools Are Very Important 142

Insight 34: Never Confuse Brains with a Bull Market 142

CHAPTER SEVEN: IMPORTANT CONTEMPLATIONS 145

Insight 35: Fixer-up Property 147

Insight 36: Have Several Systems for Buying Property 151

Insight 37: How to Make Money in a "No Growth Economy," 153

Insight 38: Pricing for a Fast and Profitable Sale 155

Insight 39: Property Management Can Make or Break You 163

Insight 40: Know Your Local & State Government Regulations 169

Insight 41: Holding Title 172

Insight 42: Good Insurance Protects Your Assets 174

Putting It All Together and Creating a Game Plan 177

My Pillars and Insights 181

Mortgage and Real Estate Terms Glossary 187

ACKNOWLEDGEMENTS

To everyone that has helped with this publication I want to say Thank You Very Much, your help has been greatly appreciated. I would especially like to say Thank You to the hundreds of customers and friends who I've have been fortunate to meet and conduct business with over the years. I sincerely hope that they have learned, profited and enjoyed it as much as I have.

The investors that I have been privileged to work with have been instrumental in helping me to develop my *Pillars and Insights for Real Estate Investing*. They have been very generous in sharing their ideas as I have shared ours with them. It has been a very profitable relationship for all of us and I hope it will continue for many more years.

I would like to especially thank Connie Garrett, my spouse, who has been a huge help and a source of encouragement while I was writing this book. She carried extra responsibilities and burdens while I was busy working on it.

I would like to thank Mr. Charles Baker and Mr. Dick Geehan for their valuable input and time spent helping with this publication.

A big thank you to the National Association of REALTORS®, which was very generous and timely with its help and providing appropriate data as needed.

I really appreciate the help of Mrs. Orva Rothgeb, the greatest sister anyone could ever hope to have.

A NOTE TO READERS

This material will teach you when is the best time to invest in real estate and how to do it. Perhaps the most important part for you is that you will learn which properties will make the best investment. I have benefited from this information, my friends and customers have benefited, and I sincerely hope that you will benefit from it. Now is the time for you to start putting this material to use. Don't delay: start forming your action plans now as you read this material. What is it that you need to accomplish to buy your first home, a larger home or perhaps an investment property? Is it repairing your credit, accumulating money, getting a better job, meeting with a loan officer or REALTOR®? Perhaps it is the biggest item of all: *dealing with the fear of the unknown?*

A lot of us are so busy making a living we do not devote enough time to making any real money. Understand that you will need to step out of your normal comfort zone to realize your financial dreams. You must take action and yes, you must be willing to assume responsibility for additional risk; every investment requires a certain degree of risk. Experience and education will greatly reduce the level of risk, fear and increase the probability of success. *Education is an extremely powerful tool if you put it to use.*

This material will provide a step-by-step plan showing you exactly how to get started and keep on track. The hardest part is getting started. Maybe it will help you to realize that millions of families and individuals have been through this process. If they were able to accomplish their goals, you know that you can also accomplish yours. If you need encouragement or help, send us an e-mail and let us help you to get moving toward your dreams. Homes are not going to become cheaper in the future. They are going to continue appreciating and it will become harder and harder to purchase a home: land, material and labor costs will continue to increase as the population of this country increases.

This is not a "Get Rich Quick," nor is it a "Zero Down Scheme." This is a realistic approach that the average person or family can use to maximize their return on their real estate investment. It is a "Common Sense" approach that will work for you in all types of markets. It can change your financial future for the better. When it comes to great real estate you are going to learn how to find it, buy it, manage it, and sell it for a substantial profit.

To give you some information about myself, I studied economics and business. I was a licensed Real Estate Broker for 32 years, and am a licensed Mortgage Broker. I have been investing in real estate since 1972. I have invested in bare land, farm ground, apartments and single family homes, and I have worked with hundreds of investors as a REALTOR® and as a mortgage banker.

I would like to make a point of disclosing that I am not a professional writer; in fact I have never tried to publish any of my writings and this book was simply an act of passion on my part. I am passionate about sharing with people ideas about the correct way to invest in real estate.

Larry Garrett
Branch Manager for a Mortgage Banker
azmortgageman@cox.net

CHAPTER ONE

THE EIGHT PILLARS

I will begin by explaining my eight "Pillars" of purchasing real estate followed by my separate and additional "Insights" of real estate investing. If you have the desire and interest to invest in real estate, reading this book will be a great place to get you started in the right direction. I have been investing in real estate since 1972, and I have learned a few things about the business which I would like to share with you. I have done many things the wrong way (hard and expensive) and a few things the right way (better and cheaper). I have made money on nearly all of my real estate investments and yes, I have lost money on a few. As with any investment program, you can lose money investing in real estate. One thing that was important to me was to learn from my experiences and improve on my performance. You can learn a lot from my trial and experiences and those of other real estate investors without incurring the costs of that education.

I believe it is a lot easier to get started and be successful at investing today than it has been in the past. There is more information available today because of technology; it is fast, accurate, cheaper to obtain and much of it is absolutely free. This will be discussed in more detail in Chapter Four.

There are also many more types of loan products available *at historically low interest rates*. If you have good credit and adequate reserves there are probably several loan products available to help you finance your purchase of real estate.

Single family homes are the easiest and simplest real estate in which to invest for most individuals; besides, everyone needs a place to live. A single family home gives the greatest return on your investment, requires less time, less money and is the simplest investment to make in real estate. Let's start with why you may want to invest in real estate.

Advantages of owning real estate

1. Owning your own home should provide a higher quality of life with much more personal satisfaction versus collecting a drawer full of rent receipts.
2. You will build up equity. If you put 10% down on the purchase of a house and that

house appreciates at 8%, the appreciation is based on the total value of the property, not just on the down payment. Also, you are probably going to be forced to save by paying down the principal on your mortgage.
3. Owning your own home gives you financial leverage. You can buy property with a very small down payment, or possibly, no down payment at all. When you borrow, you are using "other people's money" and taking advantage of financial leveraging.
4. If you buy the right home in the right neighborhood it should appreciate. It is absolutely critical to buy in an area that is appreciating as fast as possible, now and in the future.
5. If you are purchasing investment properties, depreciation is a non-cash write-off that will enable you to lower your annual taxable income by allowing you to lower the value of buildings and equipment for income tax purposes.
6. You will be reducing the amount of money you must pay towards your State and Federal income taxes because you can deduct interest and property taxes paid on your owner occupied home and a vacation home. Plus, you get to take depreciation on your investment properties and deduct all appropriate business expenses.
7. Income may be generated from "positive cash flow" on rental properties.
8. Equity build-up is the most important reason that I invest. Where can the average American family invest their money and get as great a return on their investment as they can on real estate? You can truly become rich with your real estate investments. I have seen estimates that show 95% of the average American family's total wealth at their time of retirement came from their real estate investments.

If you purchase residential real estate in a growing area, it is not hard to make money over the long term on your investment. I personally have not saved a dime in my entire life from the wages that I have earned over the years. It is extremely hard to get ahead in America today just by accumulating savings from your personal income. Why? If you do not own real estate today you are paying a lot of your income towards State and Federal income taxes. About the only deductions available to a regular W2 employee are personal deductions for yourself, your spouse, your children and interest and property taxes paid on real estate that you may own.

Most families in America are simply not going to get ahead today if they do not own real estate. *This material will teach you how to maximize your return on your investment.* I have developed a set of rules or axioms that I follow when contemplating the purchase of property.

THE EIGHT PILLARS

Hopefully, these axioms will help you get started in the right direction and help keep you on a fun and profitable road without incurring many of the learning trials and costs that I incurred. *Mistakes cost you time and money and you need to avoid them as much as possible. Yes—investing in real estate can indeed be fun and profitable, if it is done properly.*

I am not providing legal or accounting advice in this publication. Consult your attorney or CPA for legal or accounting advice. *If you are contemplating the purchase of investment property, the first purchase you should make is a current copy of your state's landlord/tenant laws.* Learn the appropriate laws and follow them to the letter; remember that tenants have legal rights that must be recognized. You need to know your landlord/tenant laws before you begin investing.

There are many investors in real estate and many different approaches. They vary from buying properties at foreclosure sales, tax sales, fixer-ups, flipping, etc. Most of these require a lot of money, time, work and a high degree of risk. Most of these should be left to the full-time experienced pros that have access to working capital, time and the resources to work with these types of properties.

You are dealing with too many potential and expensive unknowns with these types of properties. I have known and worked with many investors that have been involved with these various programs. Some of them made money during hot market conditions, but most eventually lost everything as soon as the housing market slowed down, which it always does.

Buying properties and fixing them up for a quick resale may sound exciting at cocktail parties, but if the market changes from a "hot market" to a "dead market" (it always does), you could be financially wiped out, very quickly. Owning two or three vacant houses plus your owner occupied house that you have invested your life savings into can turn a "dream adventure" into a "financial nightmare." This material will teach you a *"Common Sense Way to Invest"* which will minimize nearly all of the most common mistakes that real estate buyers or investors make.

Really, it is not that hard to make sound investment decisions with common sense guidelines.

I am going to explain how to invest in just about any type of market and make money during the process. Yes, you must use different investment approaches in different types of markets and in different market locations. First, I divide the U.S. market into two major markets, the coastal states and the central part of the U.S. In my opinion these two major markets require different approaches to buying and selling real estate. We will cover both markets and how to deal with their individual situations.

In my mortgage business I have very active clients in both types of markets. I will give you real examples of how they conduct their business in the different markets. *You should find it very interesting in how the markets are so different. Also, I conduct my real estate investment business differently in a very active market verses a slow market.*

You always need to understand that all market conditions are temporary and will change very dramatically in the future. *The only constant in the markets is change; change never stops in any market.* That is probably the biggest mistake made in investing; people always assume the market is going to continue to go up, or it is always going to continue to get worse. Of course, neither is ever correct.

Everything changes but change itself.

– JOHN F. KENNEDY

The real questions are *how long will the market continue moving in its current direction* and *how far will it move in the opposite direction*? Let's look at how to determine somewhat accurate answers for these questions. No one can give you absolute answers, and if they try to convince you that they know the answers, my advice is run, don't walk, in the other direction. I have developed a set of Pillars and Insights that will guide you in your investment program and is organized entirely different than any real estate investment book that I have ever read. If you are a first time homebuyer or an experienced professional you can use this material to help guide you in your purchase decisions. If you are a long term investor, a flipper, into new homes, fixer-ups, or whatever, these axioms will provide you with valuable guidance. Whenever I am contemplating the purchase or sale of real estate, I always refer back to these concepts.

THE EIGHT PILLARS

My "Pillars" and "Insights" for successful real estate investing with the specific goals of minimizing maintenance and management costs while maximizing long term appreciation and limiting selling costs.

PILLAR I

You should be Excited and Enthusiastic about Investing in Property to Have Fun and Be Successful.

Think of real estate as a sole proprietorship business. It is your business and you need to manage it as a business. Many people are comfortable with the idea of running their own business, dream about having their own business, and live for the time that they can become their own boss. You can accomplish this with real estate by starting out part-time and gradually working into full-time, if that is your goal. Others are terrified of the idea, or are just not interested and do not want to be bothered. However, everyone should, at the very least, own their own home.

If you get excited about the idea of investing in real estate either as a home owner or as an investor, but hold back because you don't know where or how to begin, these concepts will be a real learning experience for you. If you take the time to read this material and understand it, you will be much more comfortable in making a purchase decision regarding real estate. The more you know, the more logical and profitable decision you should be able to make.

The real secret of success is enthusiasm. Yes, more than enthusiasm, I would say excitement. I like to see men get excited. When they get excited they make a success of their lives.

– WALTER CHRYSLER

PILLAR 2

You need to be Able to See the Long Term Potential in a Property Before Buying.

Location is not everything in real estate, but it is extremely important. You want to buy property that other people will want to purchase from you in the future. If I am contemplating purchasing a house (even as my personal residence), my first consideration is whether the property is going to make a good long term investment. If I am not convinced of its investment potential, I simply will not consider purchasing the property. I want property that will be in demand 5, 10 or 20 years into the future.

Most buyers of homes, especially first time buyers, are more focused on how much cash they will need and how much their monthly payments will total. These are important considerations, I agree, but how many truly consider the long term investment potential of the property? This is the largest financial investment that most people will ever make in their entire lives; buyers need to be able to determine which properties will provide the greatest return on their investment.

In my 35 years experience in the business, as a REALTOR® and for the last 30 years as a lender, I can only remember a few home buyers who placed any consideration on the investment potential of the property. Sophisticated, long term investors, on the other hand, base most of their buying decision upon the investment potential of the property.

Just imagine, if the average home in the USA appreciates 1 to 2% above the rate of inflation with virtually "no consideration" by the average buyer about its investment potential, how much more could you increase your appreciation by logically analyzing the investment potential of a property before buying? It's like throwing a dart at the investment section of the newspaper to decide which company you are going to invest your retirement account in versus trying to make a logical analysis to determine which company would make the best long term investment. You are going to learn how to analyze property for its long term potential. *After you learn and use the material in this book you will never look at a residential home in the same light again.*

The successful man is one who had the chance and took it.

– ROGER BABSON

THE EIGHT PILLARS

PILLAR 3

The 20/20/60 Rule; Buy Smart, Sell High, Manage Well.

You need to learn how to analyze a property for its long term potential and how to buy it correctly: you will learn how to do that as you read this material. There are several steps to go through in the process. *You must make it a priority to manage the property professionally.* The management of the asset is every bit as important as purchasing the right property in the right area. We will go step by step on how to manage your property. If you do not know how or do not want to manage property, you must hire a professional property manager to insure that it is done properly and legally. There are some excellent property managers with years of experience available in the business. Proper property management will also be discussed in detail in this book. Finally you need to know when and how to sell the property to maximize your return from the asset. **I call this my 20/20/60 Rule: 20% is buying at the right time and price, 20% is selling at the right time and for the maximum amount, and 60% is managing the property correctly.** You will learn when and how to deal with all three from this material.

Small opportunities are often the beginning of great enterprises.

– DEMOSTHENES

PILLAR 4

Maximize Your Appreciation: Stay Close to Centers of Employment.
If Local Employment is Increasing, Property Values are Increasing.
If Local Employment is Decreasing, Property Values will be Decreasing.

The value of a house is not determined by how much it costs to build the home. *The value is determined by the demand for housing in that local community.* Housing is a local market. Yes, there is a national market as well, but the value of a specific home is determined by a very localized market. If employment is increasing (new jobs are being created) in a community, the value of the local housing should be going up in value, or vice-versa.

In any major metropolitan area, different parts of the community will appreciate at different rates, regardless of the national market. Follow the local employment situation in your community, state, and national region. Jobs can be created in an area faster than houses can be built, or jobs can disappear faster than housing supply can be reduced in a community. Understand that once houses are built, they are going to be around for the next 50, 100, or 150 years. The amount of available housing can increase fairly easily, but it decreases very slowly.

At the same time, when housing hits a slow market, the value of homes may decline, but the drop in value is seldom more than 1% to 5%. What really happens is the number of houses selling in the local market may take a big drop. Major cities simply do not disappear off of the face of the map in the US; at least so far they never have. The three markets which have taken very serious job losses in the past have been Houston, Texas, Detroit, Michigan and Silicon Valley in California.

Houston, Texas was hit hard because of the fall in the price of oil during the early 1970's. That market seems to have recovered at this time. Detroit, Michigan has been on a decline in jobs and population for a long time due to the automobile industry. Silicon Valley's market loss was because of the dot com collapse in the 1990's. Silicon Valley lost over 900,000 jobs in a fairly short time period. This represents the largest job loss ever to have occurred in the US. Despite a huge loss of employment in these communities, all of them have survived, and I am sure will prosper again. Houston has already recovered and is developing a more diversified economy. The point is that even as local jobs disappeared and housing was devastated, eventually the markets established new levels of equilibrium. However, as a property owner or as an investor, these types of job declines are not what you want to experience. You want markets that are experiencing job creation, now and well into the future.

PILLAR 5

Buy into Growth Areas, Stay Close to Freeways, Schools, Jobs and Shopping Centers.

It is not hard to tell when you are driving through a community that is growing and prospering. It may be not be obvious as to why it is prospering, but you can look around and see new housing sub-divisions, new shopping centers and new freeways. These are features of a community that is on the move. You can also be assured that it is a community that is creating new jobs, lots of new jobs. Values will be increasing in both residential and commercial properties. There will be more demand for housing in the community than what is available and that demand will continue as long as new jobs are being created.

Next you must determine the quality and the source of job creation in the local area. Is it long-term quality growth in a diversified economy or is it a single industry economy that may decline or disappear at some point in the future? You always want as much diversification as possible in the local markets. You also want to see growth in income in the local markets. Increases in the employee's income are extremely important. I will show how to easily measure this growth later in the book. Let's take one step at a time so that it will all come together at the end.

PILLAR 6

"The Yield Curve" is the Best Leading Indicator.

"The Yield Curve" is the best leading indicator of future economic activity; it is correct over 80% of the time. No other measurement has been as accurate at determining future turning points in the economy. The yield curve is not produced by the government or any private organization. It is a product of the financial markets, and reflects the opinions of investors on the direction of the economy and inflation. The curve shows you what bond traders expect of future economic activity, inflation and future interest rates.

The Yield Curve is used to "time" your purchases and sales. You want to buy in a weak market and sell in a strong market. This can be as important as "location" for your investment program. A yield curve shows how bond rates vary from short-term versus long-term bonds. A yield curve will show a rate for three month treasuries, 6 months, 1 year 2, 5, 10 and up to 30 years; the longer the money is committed, the higher the yield rate that the investor will normally want on his money.

The investor's concern is that the rate of inflation may go up at some point in the future in addition to all the other unknown risks that may come up over the years. The Federal Reserve sets short term interest rates, but long term rates are established by the open markets. This is important; be aware that the value of real estate nationally increases at a rate of 1 to 3% above the rate of inflation. If inflation is higher than 2%, the Fed may increase the short term interest rates to slow economic activity. If the rate of inflation is less, the Fed may lower short term interest rates to increase economic activity.

Inflation decreases the value of cash holdings by lowering its future purchasing power. It also increases the value of real estate holdings. Real estate is a great hedge against future inflation since it appreciates at a higher rate than the rate of inflation. Your mortgage is locked into current dollars but will be paid back with future dollars that will have a lower purchasing power than current dollars.

The Yield Curve is going to be discussed in much more detail in Insight #9 "The Yield Curve, Better Than a Crystal Ball." This concept is very important to understand and follow. Understanding the Yield Curve will help you in all types of investment products such as stocks, bonds, mutual funds, and annuities. Its use is not just limited to investing in real estate.

PILLAR 7

Location, Location and Location.

The location of your property is established at the time of purchase. Nothing is more important than location when it comes to determining the future value of real estate. A lot of features about real estate can be changed. Those changes may require spending a lot of money and time, but they can be changed. Location cannot be changed; the property is always going to be located in the same place.

As a buyer you have the luxury and responsibility of deciding in which area you prefer to purchase property. Once you have purchased a house, you are going to be stuck with that location as long as you own the property. Make a wise and informed decision; it is absolutely critical that you buy in the best location that you can afford.

The desirability of a location changes for the better or worse with time. You want your property's location to work for you, not against you. A single family home in a great location is only going to go up in value. Buy a single family home in a bad location and you have bought yourself a series of management headaches and a financial black hole.

Location is going to work for you and make you money or it is going to work against you and cost you time and money. Poor property location is one of the common mistakes that new investors make when purchasing investment property. They start out buying the least expensive property that they can locate for investment purposes. There is always a reason why a property in one area is cheaper than a similar one in another area. Do not start out buying someone else's headaches. If you start down the wrong path at the beginning, how are you going to get on the right path?

PILLAR 8

Timing is extremely Important.

Do not fight the markets; let the market work in your favor. There are good times to be buying and excellent times to be selling. Learn to think for yourself; avoid the herd instinct. The best time to buy is when the market is down, and the best time to sell is when the market is hot. It is a very simple concept that every one understands but most people do not practice.

If you have ever tried to sell a house in a slow market, you understand how frustrating it can be to fight the markets. At the same time, if you have ever sold a house in a hot market you can understand how amazing it can be to have buyers fighting each other to buy your house.

I have sold in both types of markets and neither one of them are indicative of a healthy market.

I have learned as a buyer I want to buy in slow markets, and as a seller I want to sell in a hot market. I have also learned that neither market situation is going to last very long in a healthy economy.

It is not hard to tell when you are in either market, just look at the newspaper headlines. They are either reporting about the market crashing or about how fast the market is appreciating and that it is going to create a market bubble. In either case, the conclusion is that homeowners are going to incur huge financial losses.

The actual truth is that neither scenario is correct. The market value of homes does not crash, the number of homes sold decreases, but the value of those homes sold is very close to their true market values. Housing bubbles can be defused very quickly by the Federal Reserve System without destroying property values.

Follow the Yield Curve and interest rates and plan to buy or sell according to local market conditions. Do not get into a market situation where you have to sell in a slow market, it can be brutal. I plan my purchasing activities 12 to 24 months ahead of the time I am going to be buying. Those plans are based on what I believe the market is going to be like for the next 5 or 6 years.

My selling plans for property are planned years ahead of the actual selling times. I may own the property through several market swings before I actually sell. I have other properties that I have no intention of ever selling in my life time. I will probably let the next generation fight those battles. Hopefully, they will have read this book by that time so that they will have some idea as to what to do and when to do it.

It is always more important to be able to sell than it is to buy.

QUICK REVIEW

1. You need to be excited about real estate investing to be successful at it. Knowledge and experience will make you more comfortable with the process.
2. You need to be able to see long term potential in a property, now and in the future. Is it property that will be in demand 5, 10 or 15 years into the future?
3. Buy smart, sell high and manage well. All are extremely important aspects of your investment program.
4. Stay close to centers of employment. If local employment is increasing, property values will be increasing. If local employment is decreasing, property values will decrease.
5. Buy into growth areas. The stronger the local economy, the better your investment will perform for you over time.
6. The Yield Curve is the best predictor of future economic activity. Interest rates are an extremely important component of real estate investing; do not get caught off guard by a change in the rates.
7. *Location* is determined by the buyer at the time of purchase, and it either will work for them or against them as long as they own the property. Location will have a huge affect on the rate of appreciation, the ease of management and the salability of the property.
8. Timing is extremely important; keep your eye on the local markets for which direction they are going and why. Timing should be determined by market forces, buy into slow markets and sell into hot markets. Timing affects the costs of the property at the time of purchase, and it affects the net proceeds at the time of sale. Flow with the markets, do not fight the markets. Don't swim against the current.

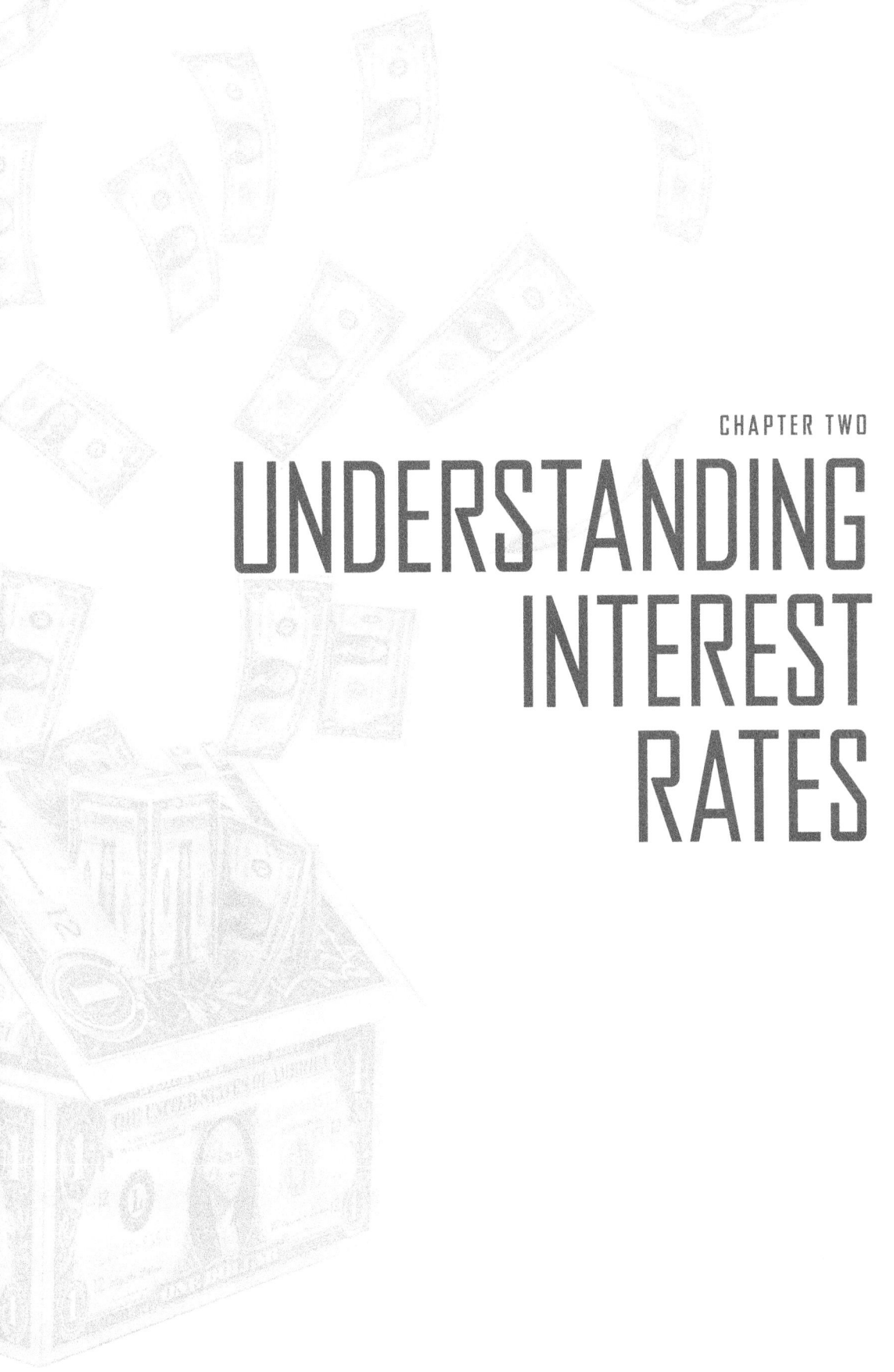

CHAPTER TWO

UNDERSTANDING INTEREST RATES

INSIGHT 1

Do Not Fight the Feds.

Over the last 4 or 5 years many people who considered themselves sophisticated investors have been able to buy single family homes, fix them up and then flip (sell them) for a fast profit. This can work very well in a market that is appreciating at an extremely high rate; say 15% to 30% per year. The high rate of appreciation can compensate for a lot of bad decisions that were made during the process of purchasing, rehabilitating and the marketing of the property.

Sooner or later, the market is going to switch from a "hot market," to a "slow market," and back to a "normal market". When this happens, the investors may not be able to sell their inventory or properties in a timely manner. I have seen markets where you could sell anything in a matter of a few days. Buyers would be fighting each other to make ridiculous offers on a house. Suddenly the market switches, and it could take you a year to sell the same house for a lot less money.

This kind of market swing happens quite often. What is the big factor that causes the swing? The Federal Reserve System decides that "enough is enough," and they start raising the interest rates in a very dramatic fashion. They want to control the market to prevent it from becoming overextended; they do not want to see a "bubble" build up in the housing market. This is a situation in which housing continues to inflate at a much higher rate than the market fundamentals can sustain. If housing continues to inflate at a much higher rate than borrower's income is increasing, a "bubble" in the market is created. This bubble could eventually burst and the price of housing could collapse. The Fed is going to do whatever is required to prevent that from happening. They can and will step in and calm the markets down to sustainable levels. How do they accomplish this? It is very simple; they raise the interest rates to whatever level is necessary to slow the markets down to a realistic level. They are very experienced at this and will not hesitate to raise rates very dramatically and in a very short time period. Overnight;

goodbye "hot" real estate market, hello "dead" market. The change can be extremely brutal for any homeowner who needs to sell quickly. Don't get caught in one of these market swings. You must keep an eye on interest rates and understand what is going on in the bond markets (this will be covered later in the material).

Any investor who is buying in anticipation of completing a fast sale better be prepared to hold on for the long haul just in case the property does not sell quickly. How is that done? It is very simple; the investor must be prepared to rent the property out until the market returns to a more normal level. The market will stabilize after interest rates return to more normal levels. What are normal levels? Over about the last 300 years the average interest rates have been approximately 6.88% per annum. We have been fortunate to experience interest rates below the historical averages in recent years, but that has not always been the case.

QUICK REVIEW

1. The Fed can either stimulate the economy, or slow it down, simply by raising or lowering interest rates.
2. Markets typically move from a "Normal Market," to a "Hot Market," to a "Dead Market," depending upon the level of interest rates and local employment opportunities.

INSIGHT 2

As Interest Rates Go Up, Property Values Will Decline.

The real estate market is very dependent upon interest rates. As an investor you must understand the relationship between interest rates and the demand for housing. When buyers are looking at homes to purchase, their experience is very similar to shopping for automobiles.

The automobile manufacturers learned a long time ago that price is not the major determining factor in a car purchase. The main concern is how much cash will be needed at time of purchase and if the buyer can afford the monthly payments. It is the same with real estate. Potential home buyers do not relate as much to the total price as they do to the monthly payments. It does not matter if the price is in the $200,000, $300,000 or $500,000 range. Their concern is the same. *Can I make the monthly payments?*

As interest rates go up, the monthly payment goes up very quickly. The Fed is very aware of this relationship. Consequently, if they decide they need to slow the market down, they know exactly how to do it. Raise interest rates, and the housing and automobile markets will immediately slow down.

Why does the Fed want to slow the market down? The Federal Reserve System was established by Congress to promote the *goals of maximum employment, stable prices, and moderate long-term interest rate.* They accomplish this by lowering the demand for products and services by raising short-term interest rates. As interest rates go up, the demand for nearly all products and services will dramatically decline. As the demand drops, our national economy will slow down, particularly housing and automobiles. The reason an increase in interest rates effect housing and automobiles so much is because those items are very capital intensive industries. It takes large amounts of money to finance the construction of housing and the purchase of housing. Plus, the financing of the purchase of homes ties up capital for several years. The average loan is written for a time period of 30 years. Loans are now starting to appear in the markets that are written for 40 or 50 years. Several decades back the normal loan was written for 15 years, and then it went to 20 years, 30 years, and now 40 or 50 years.

The purpose of extending the loans was to keep the monthly payment as low as possible as the price of homes kept increasing. The price of homes will continue increasing in the future because the price of land, labor and materials will continue to rise. In October of 2006, the population of the US first reached 300,000,000 people. By 2040, the population is projected to reach 400,000,000. That is a 33% increase in our population in only 34 years. Did you know that the U.S. is the third largest country in the world in regards to total population? We are only surpassed by China and India. All of these people will have one thing in common: they will need a place to live and raise their families.

In 2006, single women made up 18% of home purchases, single men 11%, unmarried couples 7%, and less than 50% make up the typical family of husband, wife and children. How can existing housing not go up tremendously in value? Housing is going to continue being a wonderful investment opportunity as long as the investor uses a little common sense. In fact, I think it is going to become an even better long term investment in the future than it has been in the past.

We have said that as interest rates go up, property values tend to flatten out or decline. As interest rates go down, property values go up, very dramatically. This is one of the reasons why property values increased so dramatically during the 2000 to 2005 time periods. Interest rates were at historically low rates during that time period. In Oct. 2003, interest rates reached a 40 year low of 5% for a 30 year fixed mortgage.

Property values across the U.S. climbed dramatically because of historically low interest rates that were available for the purchase of homes. Some markets on both coasts were experiencing 30% to 50% appreciation per year. That rate is not sustainable because it was increasing faster than peoples' income was increasing. Thus, in 2006 most of the markets came to a screeching halt, as the Fed raised interest rates 19 times in 24 months. The rate increases were put in place to slow down the rate of inflation that we were experiencing at the time. The rate of inflation was as high as 4%, and the Fed have made it very clear that they do not want long term inflation to exceed 2% per annum. Towards the end of 2006, the Fed stopped raising rates because they thought they were gaining control over the rate of inflation. Interest rates will be discussed in more detail in Insight #8. Just remember that as rates go up property values may decline, as rates drop property values normally go up.

UNDERSTANDING INTEREST RATES

Property Values from 1971 to 2006

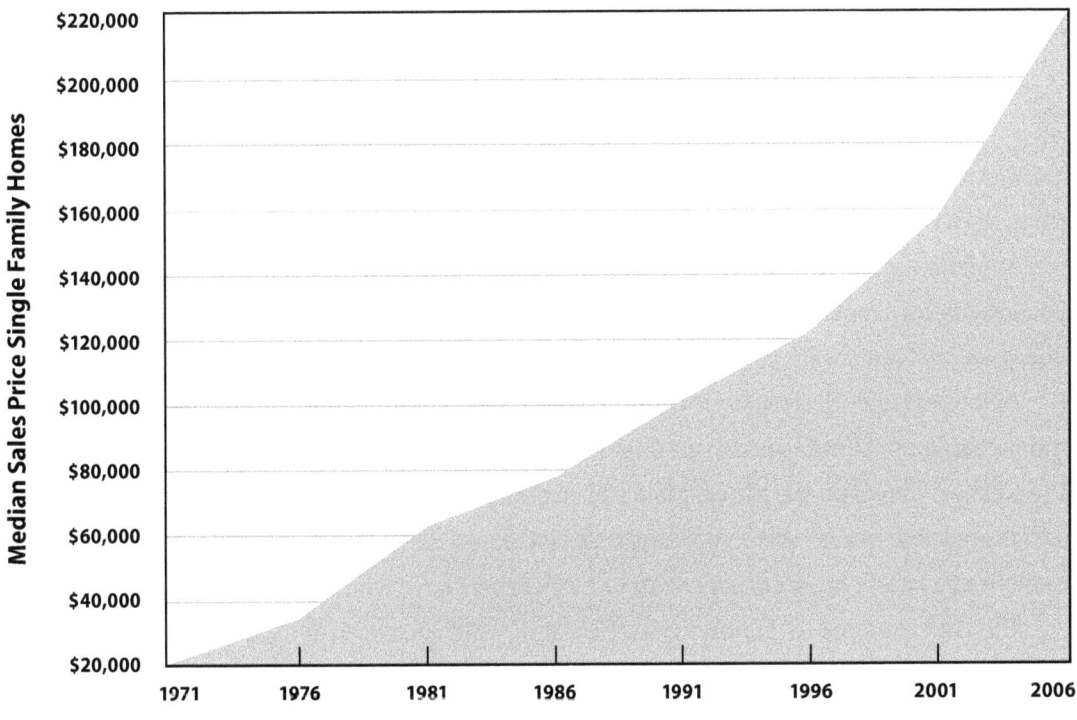

Source: National Association of REALTORS®

QUICK REVIEW

1. The real estate market is very dependent upon interest rates.
2. Buyers are normally mostly concerned about the amount of cash required to purchase and the amount of their new monthly payment.
3. As interest rates go up, property values will decline. As rates decline, property values will dramatically increase.

INSIGHT 3

As Interest Rates Increase, Rents Will Increase; as Rates Decline, Rents Will Decline.

As interest rates increase, fewer investors will be out actively purchasing additional rental properties, thus eventually a shortage of available rental properties will develop. That means that landlords of current rental properties can charge more rent for their existing properties. If you already own rental properties, an increase in interest rates is not necessarily bad news since you know that rents will be rising.

As interest rates decline, housing temporarily becomes more affordable, consequently more people can afford to purchase their own homes. As more investors enter the market and the supply of rental properties dramatically increase, the pool of available tenants decreases and the number of available rental properties increases. Rents will decline, and it will take longer to rent a vacant property even with reduced rents.

This is an example of "Supply versus Demand" which occurs in all aspects of a free economy. Rental properties are subject to the same market forces that all other businesses experience in the market place. The experienced investor must be aware of this market phenomenon and plan for it.

One way of preparing for changes in demand for rentals is to lease your properties on long term leases; a lease is a rental period of 12 months or more. I have rented many of my properties for two or three years at a time. In fact, most of my tenants stay in the same property for three to five years.

I have found that people hate to move. If I treat them right and do not try to gouge them on rents, they will stay for a long time. Sometimes, my rents are below market rates, but I do not have the expense of a vacant house and advertising for a new tenant.

If rents start to decline, I minimize my vacancy rate. I seldom have to be concerned with trying to find a qualified tenant during a market downturn. Long term, this is a win-win situation for the tenants and for me.

I am a fanatic about my rental properties being in as good a shape as possible. I would not hesitate to live in any of my rental properties myself; they all are in excellent condition. That is how I measure the condition of my properties *"Would I be willing to live in that house in its current condition?"* If the answer is "no," I get someone working on that property immediately. It does not matter what the problem is, it will be fixed.

UNDERSTANDING INTEREST RATES

Scarcity is what economics is about.

- ANON

QUICK REVIEW

1. As interest rates increase, rents will increase because of a limited amount of available rental properties and a larger pool of tenants who can not purchase at the higher rates.
2. As rates decline, housing becomes more affordable and more people can afford to buy, thus market rents tend to decline.
3. Lease your properties on long term leases (at least one year minimum).
4. Make sure that your properties are always in excellent condition.

INSIGHT 4

How the Federal Reserve Bank Affects Your Investment Program.

The Federal Reserve System was created by Congress in 1913 for the purpose of regulating our banking system and controlling the amount of money in circulation. The Federal Open Market Committee meets eight times a year to make decisions in regards to short-term interest rates by setting what is called the Federal Funds Rate.

When you read about the Fed changing rates, it is the Federal Funds Rate that has changed. By law, the Fed's job is to "promote effectively the goals of maximum employment, stable prices and moderate long term interest rates."

The key parts of that statement are stable prices and moderate long-term interest rates. The Fed maintains stable prices by limiting the rate of growth and by stimulating growth when needed. They accomplish this by controlling the short term interest rates. Higher rates slow the economy, and lower rates stimulate the economy.

Prior to Chairman Paul Volcker becoming the Fed Chairman in August 1979, the bank preformed rather poorly at regulating the economy. Most of the chairmen prior to Mr. Volcker emphasized growth in the economy rather than controlling the rate of inflation, consequently, stagflation dominated the 1970's.

Stagflation meant the economy was stagnant and that inflation was out of control. Inflation peaked at 13.5 % in 1981. Under Mr. Volcker, it was successfully lowered to 3.2% by 1983 and has been fairly low ever since. The Fed under Mr. Volcker regulated the economy by raising and lowering the interest rates as needed to control inflation or to stimulate the economy.

The policies established by Mr. Volcker have been followed very closely by Mr. Allen Greenspan and the current Fed Chairman Mr. Bernanke (appointed in Feb. 2006). The chairman of the bank is appointed by the President of the U.S. for a 4 year term. In fact, most of the recent chairmen have served for several terms. Mr. Volcker served two terms, and Mr. Greenspan served for 4 1/2 terms.

The Federal Reserve Bank actually only controls short term rates by controlling the discount rate or Fed Funds rate. However, the banks throughout the banking system always follow the Fed lead.

If the Fed raises the rates, all commercial banks will immediately raise their rates. The commercial banks call their best rate the "prime rate", and it is an important benchmark that the markets follow very carefully. As the prime rate goes up, the economy starts to slow down. An increase in interest rates is felt by all businesses in the economy. Rate increases will definitely slow the economy down. Rate decreases will stimulate the economy.

Mortgage rates are closely related to the bond markets. The 10 year bond yield is a benchmark indicator that influences market interest rates. Interest rates can be very confusing and hard to understand, but they are a major factor in determining what is happening in the markets. It is imperative that you keep up on the direction that rates are moving to be able to make good decisions about investing.

No one can tell you what is going to happen to the economy, or when it will happen. However, you should always be aware of market movements and interest rates to determine which direction the economy will probably be heading. I am going to give you my interpretation of interest rates, and how I try to predict what is going to happen to the economy. Remember this is my interpretation. You need to establish your own process for predicting the direction of interest rates. There are many books available that can help you learn how to predict what direction interest rates and the economy may be moving in.

My theory is that interest rates have a fairly normal business cycle just like everything else in the business world. Most business cycles are influenced by interest rate cycles, which to a large degree are regulated by the Federal Reserve System. The main long term job of the Fed is to control and regulate the level of inflation in our economy. They lower interest rates to stimulate our economy and raise rates to slow the economy down.

When employment is high, unemployment low, and the economy is really humming along, everyone is happy. They have jobs, they are spending money which creates even more new jobs, and every thing is wonderful, correct? Well, not exactly. What is really happening is the economy is over heating. It is what economist like to call "unlimited demand for limited resources". In other words, there is too much money chasing a limited amount of resources.

So what happens? The price of everything starts to increase at a very dramatic pace. Housing and autos (for instance) start appreciating at levels that cannot be sustained because peoples' income cannot keep up with the price increases.

Inflation not only affects housing, but just about everything in our economy will suddenly start to cost more than it did a few months before, or even a few days before. Eventually, inflation can reach a point where everyone is buying just because they are afraid if they don't buy now, they will have to pay more in the near future for the same products. *Excessive inflation is simply an unjustified fear of future price increases caused by current excessive demand for limited resources.*

Eventually, the "bubble" will burst and everything could come crashing down. The economy will head in the opposite direction, and many people will lose their jobs, their houses, their stock portfolio, and the "good times come to an abrupt end," to say the least. That's why the Fed was created, to protect us from humanity's unlimited demands upon the earth's very limited and very overworked resources.

I think of interest rates in a 5 to 6 year cycle. In 1978 rates started to increase until 1981, when mortgage rates peaked at an all time high of 21% for a first mortgage. It was like trying to buy a house and financing it by paying for it with a credit card. This horrible increase in inflationary pressures was an outcome of ten years of war in Viet Nam and very poor monetary policies by the Federal Reserve System. This created a market condition known as stagflation, high inflation and slow growth, the worst of all market conditions.

Then Paul Volcker (8/1979 - 8/1987) and President Ronald Reagan (1/1981 – 1/1989) decided it was time for some serious medicine for the U.S economy. Volcker raised rates to all time highs and virtually destroyed the real estate markets at the time (and a lot of other markets). The Fed became very effective at fighting inflation. *The outcome was President Reagan obtained legislation to stimulate economic growth, fight inflation, increase employment and increase national security.* In 1986, President Reagan overhauled the income tax code which eliminated many tax loopholes for the wealthy, and at the same time, exempted millions of low income people.

> *Here's to the past. Thank God it's past!*
>
> - ANON

President Reagan insisted upon increased spending for national defense that also increased our national debt, which kept interest rates at high levels during his presidency. Note! Interest rates always come down more slowly than they go up. They can go up very quickly, and that catches many people off guard.

Since 1978, if you project interest rates over 5 year cycles, you will find that they should have bottomed out in June of 2003. They actually bottomed out in October 2003 at 5% for a 30 year first mortgage. That is not bad for a 25 year time period. It could also be just pure dumb luck, but I do not think that is the case.

The Fed has done a much better job of regulating the economy over the last 25 years. Economic volatility has been at a record low for the last two decades. We have had wonderful economic leadership during this time period, and the current expansion has been going on for 5 years. It is the third longest expansion period following the 1980 and 1990 expansions.

You need to understand that many things can influence interest rates. Money is a commodity just like gold, silver and pork bellies. Like any commodity, the more of it that is available, the less it costs. The cost of money is reflected in the rate of interest charged to borrow the money. The more abundant the supply of money, the lower the interest rate should be for the borrower.

The largest users of borrowed money are consumers, governments and corporations. These three components of our economy compete with each other for borrowed monies. This demand, or lack thereof, determines the rate of interest in the market place. The higher the demand for borrowed money, the higher the interest rates the market will demand. The U.S. Government is a huge user of borrowed money, especially when it gets involved in one of the many wars that it seems unable to avoid. If the government gets involved in a war, you can bet that interest rates will be increasing. The government will need to borrow the funds to finance the war effort, so the demand for money will always go up in a war situation.

Back to the cycles in interest rates: since 1981 rates have consistently dropped to a new low at the end of each cycle. They go back up for a 2-3 year time period, then down to a new low that was lower than the previous low. In Oct 2003, mortgages rates were lower than they had been in about the previous 40 years. People with substantial amounts of money in the banks were crying the blues because they were only getting about 1% interest on their savings. There was a huge surplus of monies around the world in relation to the demand for borrowed money.

How did this happen? If you take the amount of money worldwide that transferred from one generation to the next, from day 1 till the year 1990 and add all of those sums together, that amount is less than transferred from 1990 till the year 2000. That amount will be less than what transfers from 2000 to 2006.

Standard and Poor's 500 Index for the 500 Large Firms

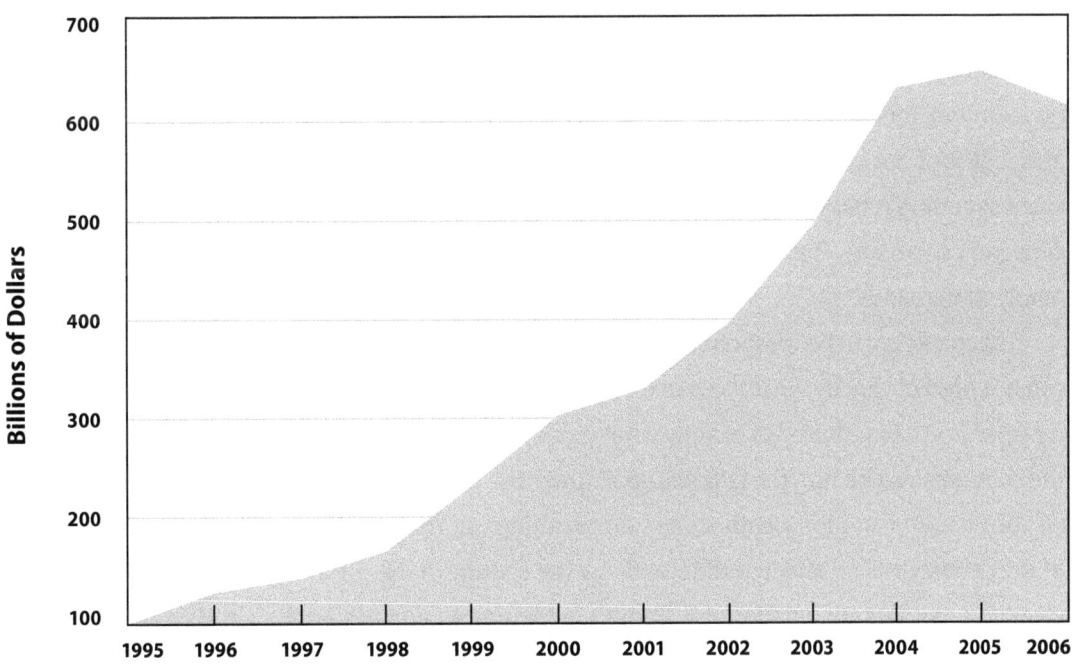

Corporations are sitting on extreme high levels of cash and cash equivalent investments.

Corporate America is drowning in liquidity. They have virtually no long term debt. They are not opening new factories, hiring new employees, or paying more dividends to the stock holders. What many are doing is buying back their own stock, to keep the price of the stock high. Buybacks help minimize the threat of being bought out by other companies.

Let's see where we are now. Money is becoming more abundant worldwide and interest rates have been declining for 25 years. This country's population is growing by leaps and bounds. Building materials, fresh water and land are becoming very scarce commodities. You figure for yourself what you think is going to happen to the price of housing over the next few decades.

You may have noticed a similarity between what I am describing in the housing market and what happens in the stock market. They both are dramatically affected by interest rates, and in fact, the two markets move in tandem with each other. What is good for housing is also great for the stock market. It seems like the stock market moves sooner and faster, either up or down, then housing. That is because the stock market is dominated by professional investors and institutions that are very aware of what is going on with interest rates and the markets. That is what they do full time, every day, all day. They must stay on top of the markets, or they will be out of business.

Our economy is divided into three major components; consumer spending or demand, government spending and capital spending by businesses. Consumer spending accounts for about 65% of our economy, government spending 19%, and capital spending 16%. Government spending is fairly stable (except during wars), and capital spending is determined by consumer spending. The consumer is the big gorilla in our economy. They are the source of nearly all demands.

The markets can be reasonably predicted if you know what to look for. However, you can not predict exactly what the market is going to do, or when. It is similar to predicting the weather. You can not predict exactly what is going to happen or when, but you can predict that the summers will be hot, the falls will cool down, the winters will be cold and icy, the springs will be beautiful and the weather will start warming up. You can also predict that different parts of the country will be affected differently by the change in the seasons. Summers in Phoenix are miserable, winters are wonderful. Summers in Minnesota are nice; winters in Minnesota are challenging.

This is similar to predicting what is going to happen to the various markets. You will never know exactly how much change to expect or exactly when, but you know there will be change and you should know in which direction it is going to be moving.

If you follow the Wall Street Journal Prime Rate that is published daily—which is available on many web sites—it is easy to follow interest rates on a daily basis. The Prime Rate is the lowest rate that the major banks charge their best customers.

If you look at the Wall Street Journal Prime Rate from January 2004 to November 2006, you should see some very interesting information. The Prime rate in Jan. 04 was 3.75% until July 04, and then the Fed started raising rates at a rate of a quarter of a percent nineteen times in a row over the next 24 months. Prime went from 3.75 % to 8.25%. That is an increase of 4.5% in approximately 24 months. That is a very large increase in interest rates and caused a very negative impact on the housing industry across the U.S.

Peaks and Valleys of the Prime Interest Rate

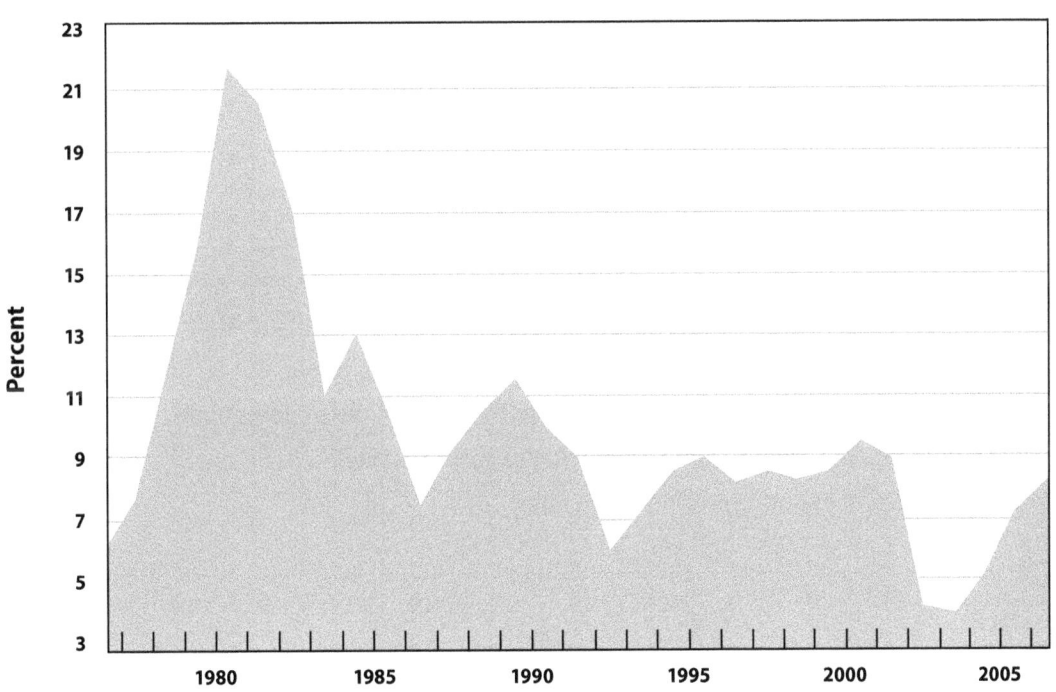

The reason that the Fed raised the rates so quickly was because the economy was extremely strong, and the rate of inflation had increased from less than 1% to about 4%. The Fed has said repeatedly that they do not want the rate of inflation to exceed 2% per annum.

They have been very adamant that if inflation gets over 2%, they are going to slow the economy down. That is exactly what they accomplished. They raised the rates and held them at a high level until the economy started slowing down. Unfortunately, raising the rates has a larger impact on housing and autos than it does on other sectors of the economy because, as we have said before, these industries are very capital intensive.

Historically, if you follow interest rates you find that the Fed normally keeps the rates at a peak level for about 6 to 12 months. Remember when I said rates decline very slowly and go up very quickly? Rates will typically peak and stay at the peak for 6 to 12 months; however, when they hit the bottom of the cycle, mortgage rates are at the very bottom for just a few hours.

Again, mortgage rates are normally based on the yield of 10 year bonds and mortgage backed securities, but that yield is going to follow the Prime Rate very closely. It should be pointed out that the Fed does not control long term rates. These rates are determined by market forces. The Feds only control short term rates, but they are very effective with the control they do exercise.

QUICK REVIEW

1. The Fed controls interest rates by controlling short term rates.
2. Anytime the rate of inflation exceeds 2%, the Fed may raise interest rates.
3. Interest rates move up and down with the business cycles.
4. The Fed does not control long term rates.

INSIGHT 5

"The Yield Curve" is better than a Crystal Ball.

I am a branch manager for a mortgage banker, and I work with investors who buy anywhere from one house per month, to one or two per year. Personally, I try to buy at least two houses per year. That is an amount that I can handle financially and have enough time available to invest in properties.

Yes! I am investing now. I am not trying to teach you something that may have worked thirty, forty or fifty years ago. I have been investing since 1970 and I plan on continuing to invest, as long as I am able to do so. I have worked with hundreds of families over the years, and I am not aware of any of them losing money on their real estate investments, either as a homebuyer or as an investor.

This program will work in any type of market, but you need to understand how interest rates change and how those changes will affect the market. You do not have to be an expert on interest rates, but you do need to know which direction they are headed and why.

Never believe that you are smarter than the market or that you have it completely figured out. You are not that smart and you will not know all there is to know. The market is the market, and it is constantly in a state of change. It does not care what you think, believe, or expect.

Surprisingly, some people are always more concerned about things that they do not have any control over and cannot prevent; for instance, a natural disaster, a terrorist attack, a meteorite, and so forth. There are "no guarantees" in life that I know about, except death and taxes. I do know that people are living longer today and that many of them who thought they were going to be taken care of financially for the rest of their lives are instead getting the shock of their lives.

Everyday you read about a company or a union that can no longer take care of their retirees, as promised. The steel workers, automobile workers and the airline employees are good examples of retired employees who thought the company was going to take care of them. Maybe it is time that workers started assuming responsibility for their own retirement versus having the company or union assume responsibility for their long term care.

Personally, I don't think many of us are going to have a choice. We either take care of ourselves or pay the consequences down the road. Real estate is an investment that can take care of you for the rest of your life, if you take care of your investment. You can do it full time or part time, whichever you prefer. I prefer doing it part time because I like what I am doing at my full time job, and I do not want all of my eggs in one basket. When I think about it, it seems strange that my part time job now makes me far more money than my full time job. The part time job will hopefully take care of me, even if I can't get out of bed in the morning.

We are going to cover what happens to the real estate markets during the various phases of interest rates cycles. I will try to make it as simple as possible, but it really is important to have good grasp on what to expect from the markets to be successful in your investment program. Remember that this information is simply to help you understand the directions and trends that you may see in the various markets cycles.

The "Yield Curve" is the best leading indicator of future economic activity because it is correct over 80% of the time. No other measurement has been as accurate in determining future turning points in the economy. The yield curve is not produced by the government or any private organization. It is a product of the financial markets, and it reflects the opinions of investors on the direction of the economy and inflation. The curve shows you what bond traders expect of future economic activity and future interest rates.

A yield curve will show a rate for three month treasuries, 6 months, 1 year 2, 5, 10 and up to 30 years. The longer the money is committed, the higher the yield rate that the investor will normally want on his money. His concern is that the rate of inflation may go up at some point in the future plus all the other unknown risks that may occur over the years. When he purchases a long term bond his potential risk is higher. The government sets short-term interest rates but long-term rates are established by the open markets. This is important! Be aware that the value of real estate normally increases at a rate slightly higher than the rate of inflation.

An increasing yield curve indicates that bond traders expect the rate of inflation to increase and consequently interest rates to rise. As rates rise, real estate activity will be diminished depending upon how much interest rates are increased. A normal yield curve will have a spread of about 2.5% between the 3 month bill and the 30 year bond rate. If the spread is greater than that, the curve is considered to be a steep curve. A steep curve is a strong indication of future inflationary pressures.

When the rate of inflation exceeds 2%, be very cautious about buying real estate because the Fed may start raising interest rates which will hold the value of new and existing housing in check.

UNDERSTANDING INTEREST RATES

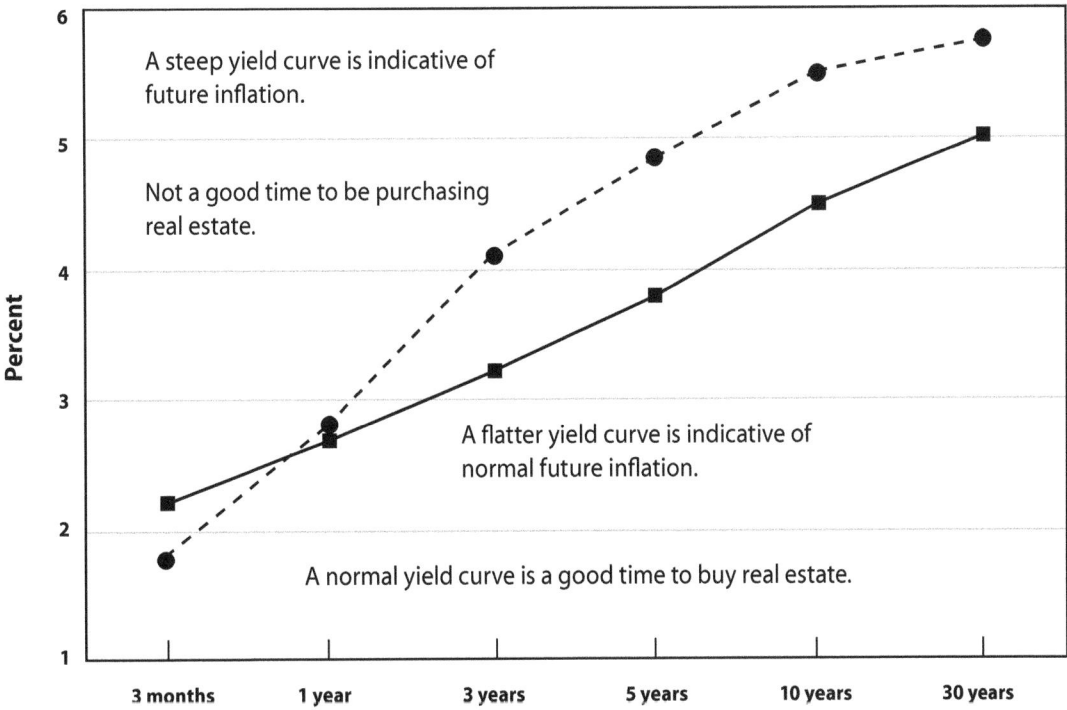

Anticipated future inflation may cause the Fed to raise rates which will decrease real estate activity.

The Federal Reserve Bank of New York calculated the probabilities of a recession based on the yield curve. When a normal yield curve is 1.2 percentage points above the 3 month bill, the chance of a recession is less than 5%.

A normal yield curve is indicative of a healthy economy and indicates that it is a good time to contemplate purchasing additional real estate.

Graph of a Flat Yield Curve

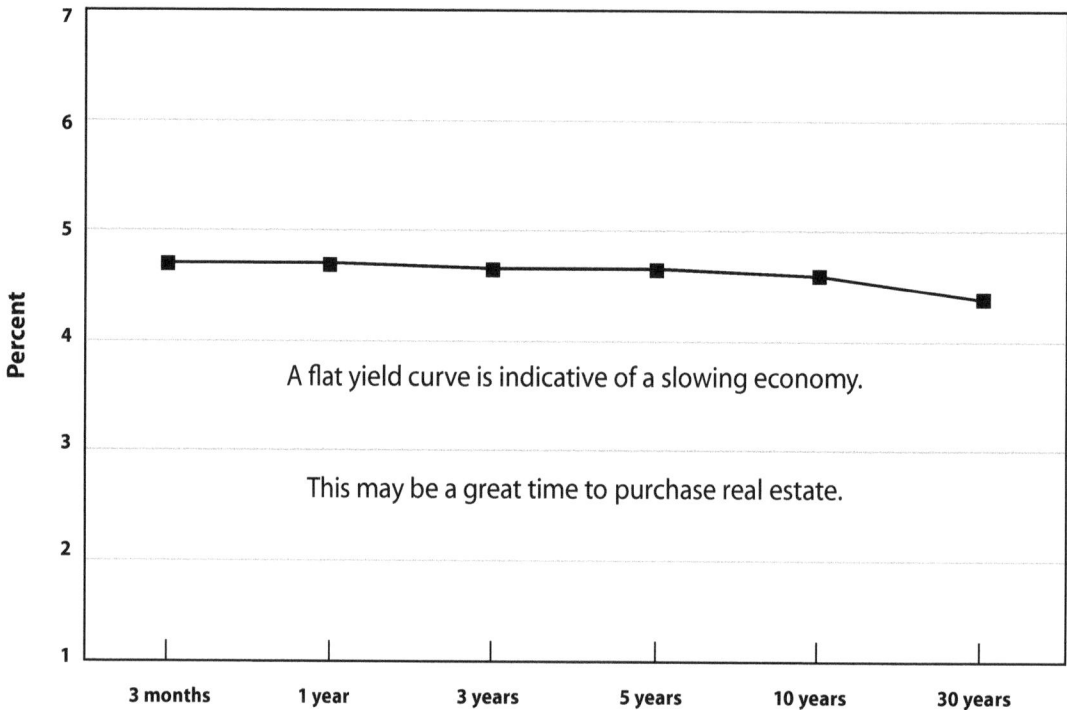

It is anticipated that future inflation will be stable and that interest rates will be declining.

A flat yield curve will show a yield that is virtually the same for each time period. In this case, the investor (the buyer of the bond) feels like the probability of inflation increasing in the future is very low. He does not think that future inflation is going to be an issue. The yields for two year, five year and ten year bonds are virtually the same. The long term investor is not expecting the economy to grow in the near future. In fact, the economy will probably decline in the near future. The probability of a recession increases to 50% when the yield curve is flat.

UNDERSTANDING INTEREST RATES

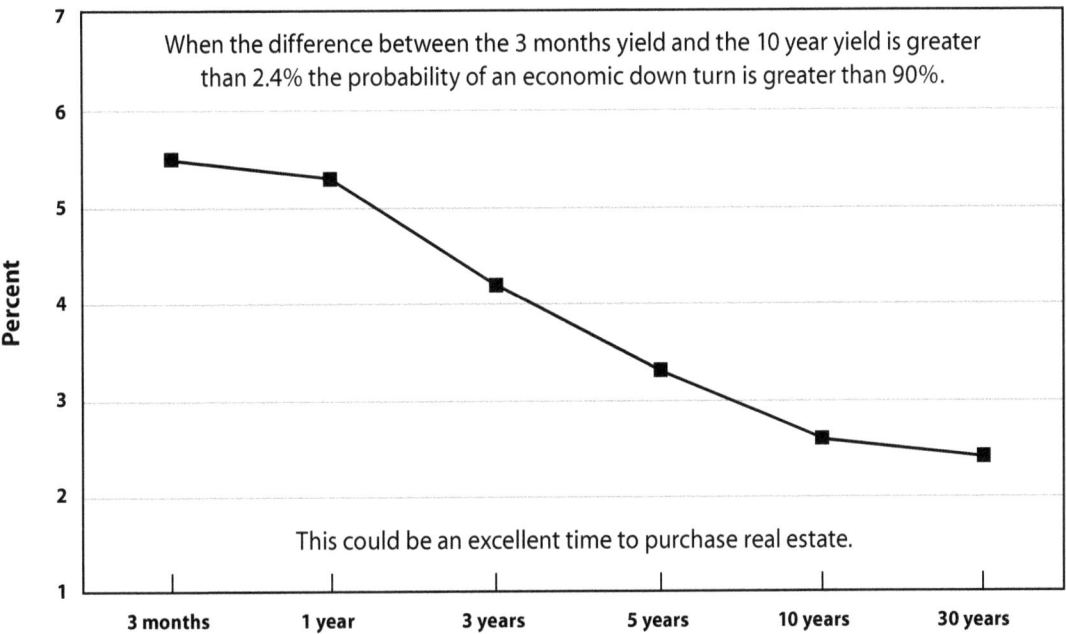

Recessions are an excellent time to buy real estate because interest rates are low and sellers are anxious.

An inverted yield curve will show that the longer the bond is written for, the lower the yield for that bond. That is because investors think that inflation is going to be lower in the future and that the amount of money available to lend will become cheaper and more abundant. An inverted yield curve indicates that the economy is headed towards a declining market situation. The economy is expected to slow down, as the demand for products and services decline. In a declining market, interest rates will decline as the economy slows. If the spread between the 3 month bill and the 30 year bond is more than 2.4 percentage points the odds of a recession within 18 months are more than 90%. This occurs when the rate on a 30 year bond is 2.4% less than the rate on a 3 month bill.

In an inverted yield market, the investor is asking for a lower yield on the longer term bonds versus the shorter term bills. The reason that the investor is willing to except a lower yield on a longer term bond is he thinks the economy is entering a recession and inflation is expected to decrease as the demand for products and services decreases.

A reverse yield curve anticipates a recession in the economy. Inflation will decrease which will lower interest rates. All six recessions since 1960 were preceded by an inverted yield curve months before the recessions. Ironically during a recession, real estate is a great investment. Interest rates are down and consumers start buying real estate. As consumers buy real estate they also start purchasing goods for their new houses. Real estate is a big factor in pulling the economy out of a recession. New home sales are a leading indicator that the economy is starting to speed up during a recession. The sales of new homes create a huge multiplier effect on the economy. Consumer purchases of new homes create jobs in construction, financial services, plumbers, electricians, home furnishings, building materials, etc. Declining new home sales is also a strong indicator of a declining economy.

Why are we covering this information in a book about real estate investing? Nationally, housing normally appreciates at 1 to 2% above the rate of inflation. Housing is also a large component of the formula that the Fed uses in calculating the rate of inflation. Notice that I said nationally, but housing has really become a local market more than a national market. Different parts of the country have drastically different real estate markets.

The different types of curves gives us an indication of what bond investors think about the direction that the markets will be moving in the future. If they demand a higher yield, it is because they expect more inflation in the future. If they accept a lower yield, they believe that inflation will be declining in the future.

Worldwide, the American dollar is the currency that investors in virtually all countries use to conduct international business, although the Euro is also gaining in influence. That is because they believe that the Fed will keep a tight rein on inflation in the U.S., which creates a more stable economy and currency. The Fed has learned how to eliminate the huge peaks and valleys in our economy. We do not go from boom to bust like we have in the past. The peaks are not as high and the valleys are not as low.

However, bond yields and interest rates have a huge impact on real estate investments, and if you want to maximize your return on real estate, you need to understand how interest rates work. You need to be able to determine which direction rates are headed, and why. You need to know that as rates increase, the market is going to slow down dramatically and stay down until the rates start declining.

If rates are declining, how long are they going to decline, and how low are they going to go? Hint, no one knows, and we can only make educated guesses, like forecasting the weather. But educated guesses are far better than sticking your head in the sand and not even trying to figure out which direction rates are headed. The Federal Government has an excellent web site which you can use to study the Yield Curve at **www.ustreas.gov/offices/domestic-finance/debt-management/interest-rate/yield.shtml**.

QUICK REVIEW

1. "The Yield Curve" is the best leading indicator of economic activity.
2. A normal curve indicates a healthy economy.
3. A flat curve indicates the economy will probably not increase and might decline in the near future.
4. An inverted curve indicates a declining market condition.
5. During a recession is an excellent time to buy real estate. There will be a lot of motivated sellers and low interest rates to finance the purchases.

INSIGHT 6

The Similarity of Tilt-A-Whirl Ride and the Economy.

I am going to use a Tilt-a-Whirl Ride to explain how six factors interact with each other to affect our economy. First, we start with the consumer. He is the 800 pound gorilla in this relationship. Consumers are responsible for 65 to 70% of all activity in the U.S. economy. The economy begins and ends with the consumer, no exceptions. The consumer creates the demand that creates our economy. As consumer demand increases, the economy increases, and visa versa.

The consumer (the gorilla) places demands on the economy. That demand stimulates the economy which eventually stimulates inflation. As inflation increases, the Fed (gorilla keeper/trainer) will step in to control inflation. The Fed raises interest rates to slow down the overheating economy. Since housing is the biggest user of credit, it gets hit the hardest by the rate increases. As rates rise, housing begins to slow down dramatically, as well as consumer demand for other products and services. As the consumers lower their demands, the economy will begin to slow down to a more sustainable level of activity.

Now we need to be able to envision this ride, not only going around and around. It is also moving up and down like a Tilt-a-Whirl at a carnival. The wave is initially created by increased demands by consumers, which is reinforced by a wave of inflation, which forces the Fed to intervene by increasing interest rates. The higher prices plus higher interest rates create a top to the wave. The wave starts receding because of a drop in demand for housing and other goods and services. We have now completed one round of the ride, and we are back where we started. The consumer (the gorilla) again starts to show his strength by buying houses and all other related goods and services.

As demand recedes, the Fed will lower rates. These lower rates will increase consumer demand. Around and around and up and down we go through the various business cycles. It takes five to six years to complete one round of the ride. During the first half of this ride the wave is moving up and then it stabilizes for about a year. The wave declines for the balance of the round.

There are a couple of things to take note of. First, nothing stays the same. Secondly, the interest rate cycle does create predictable movements in our economy. We need to be able to predict when the waves are coming, so that we can ride them. It is much easier to ride the waves than it is to swim against the current.

As an economy expands, it creates inflationary pressures. The Fed will raise rates which will slow the economy. As rates increase, consumer demand will subside, and the economy will slow.

Similarity of a Tilt-A-Whirl Ride and the Economy

30-Year Fixed Mortgage Rates

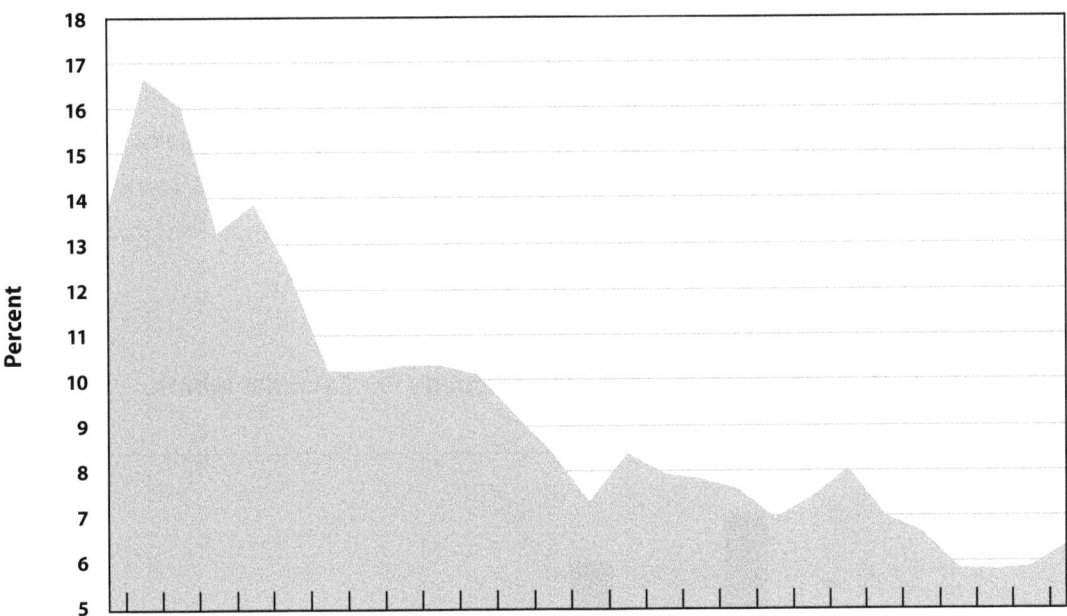

25 years of declining rates

The first thing to always remember is that as interest rates increase the value of real estate will either stabilize or decline. This graph shows how the market and interest rates interact through a normal business cycle.

It is important to realize that a business cycle can be interrupted or distorted due to circumstances beyond what would be considered a normal business cycle. A war, an act of terrorism, natural disasters or some other similar situation may distort the cycle that we would normally expect. However, do not panic. 300,000,000 people and growing will still need a place to live and work.

Everyone seems to assume that some kind of disaster will push interest rates sky high, but actually just the opposite happens. If something happens that will have a huge negative impact on the economy, the Feds immediately and dramatically lower the rates, which stimulate the economy.

There is another aspect of the market that is very important to factor into your real estate program. There is a normal cycle that real estate goes through on an annual basis. There are seasons during the year that are considered great real estate markets and seasons that are extremely slow during a normal annual market cycle.

I recommend to all of my clients to very diligently avoid having a vacant house from the first of October until the end of March. It is very difficult to rent or to sell a house during that time period.

People do not want to move during the holidays, and parents do not want their children to switch schools during a school year. In the northern parts of the country, the weather can also be a big factor in why people choose not to move during the winter months. Below is a graph showing the percentage of new homes sold per month in a calendar month. The information was calculated by averaging the numbers over a three year time period.

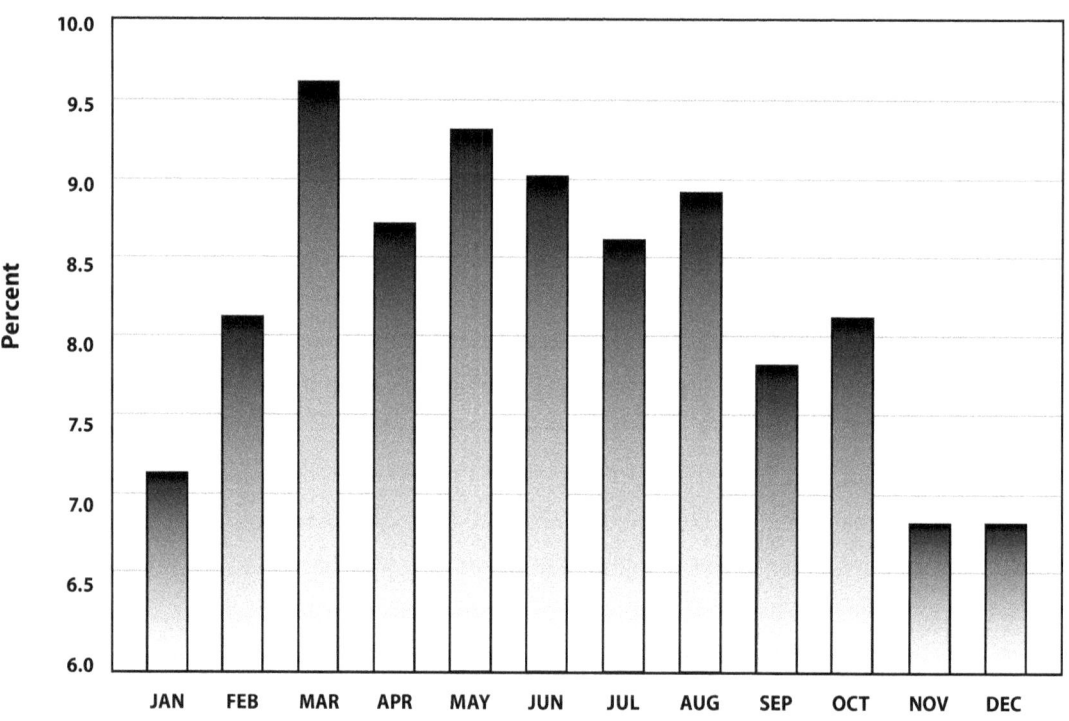

Please note November, December and January.
This concept applies to both the sale of existing homes and the renting of rental properties.

CHAPTER THREE

IMPORTANT CONCEPTS

INSIGHT 7

Newer Properties Appreciate Faster Than Older Properties.

If you track the rate of appreciation for houses, you will learn that houses appreciate faster during the first 12 to 15 years after being built, if local employment is increasing. It is very common to see appreciation rates of 10% to 15% per year for the first 15 years. Then the rate of appreciation will normally decline to about the national rate of 2% to 5% per year. This is a very important concept to be aware of, and it could have a huge effect on your return on your real estate investments.

You need to be aware that new houses bought from the builder will require large capital expenditures after you purchase the property. They will need landscaping, window coverings, ceiling fans, pools, etc. Just be aware that new houses may look like you're getting a tremendous amount of appreciation in the first couple of years, however you can spend a large amount of money on them making them livable. Of course, older houses may require time and money spent on maintenance, which may or may not increase their market value.

A word of warning, I believe, is appropriate at this time. Some first time or even experienced investors will purchase fixer-ups thinking they can do much of the repair work themselves and save money. I personally have not found that to be the case. I can hire people in the business and get the work done for about the same amount that it costs me for the materials. In other words, they can buy the materials, cover their labor costs and make a profit for about the same amount of money that the materials would cost me. Their labor is a deductible expense on investment property. An investor's labor is not deductible. Additionally, investors can continue working at their regular job. My advise is do not take time off from your regular employment to work on your investment properties thinking that you are saving money in the long run. I seriously doubt that the final numbers will look as good as you were expecting, with your total costs substantially higher and your net income lower.

QUICK REVIEW

1. Houses appreciate more quickly during the first 12 to 15 years of their life.
2. New homes require added amenities such as landscaping, pools, ceiling fans, etc. to make them livable.
3. Keep your regular job when starting your investment program.

INSIGHT 8

You Must Have Adequate and Available Reserves, Always.

Anyone can make money in a good market; you must be able to survive a bad market. If you can survive a bad market, you will make excellent money in a good market. However, you must have adequate reserves available to you at all times to be able to survive the market swings.

What are adequate reserves? That depends on each individual's financial situation and how the financing is structured on his or her properties. Ideally, you do not want to have any negative cash flow on your properties. The market rents need to be enough to cover your monthly payment, which includes principal, interest, taxes and insurance. This is very difficult to accomplish in a fast moving market without putting a lot of money down when you make your purchase, but with the right type of financing it can be accomplished. This is when you must work with an experienced Real Estate Agent and a Loan Broker that actually own investment properties themselves. Their combined experience and knowledge can be invaluable to your investment program. I believe that you should have reserves of about six months of house payments for each house and a home equity line of credit on each property.

Before everything else, getting ready is the secret of success.

- HENRY FORD

IMPORTANT CONCEPTS

I always try to maintain a Home Equity Line of Credit (HELOC) on each one of my own properties. A HELOC is a second mortgage recorded against the property. The purpose of the loan is to enable the investor to borrow against a secured line of credit when cash is needed. The HELOC is set up with a bank, and it is written for a certain loan amount. The costs of establishing the loan is very small and some banks do not charge for the loan. The investor only pays interest on the amount of money actually withdrawn from the HELOC account.

If you have a vacancy or need to make repairs, you can finance the costs by withdrawing money from the HELOC recorded against that particular property. I prefer not using the cash out of my checking account, assuming I have cash in my account. Most HELOCS are interest only payments for the first 5 years, after 5 years any balance will be amortized over 15 years. Normally you will refinance or sell during that 5 year time period; the old first mortgage and any balance on the HELOC will be combined into a new loan. The average mortgage in the U.S. is refinanced or paid off after about 3.5 years.

Financially each property should stand on its own merit. Each property should have a HELOC with a zero balance, so if you need cash for that property it is readily available. If you get into trouble with one property, such as a high negative cash flow, be prepared to dump that property. *Do not use the positive cash flow from one property to cover the loss on another.* Simply refinance if that will solve the problem, or sell it and get rid of the property. You do not want to endanger your other investment properties with one that is not working for you.

A losing property is like a rotten apple in a basket of good apples. Get rid of the bad apples before the ones next to it turn bad. Don't pull money from the HELOC on one property to cover expenses on another property. The absolute worst thing that you can do is pull money from the HELOC to pay off your personal credit cards, pay for cars, boats, vacations, etc. This type of behavior will destroy your investment program. It is the same as pulling money out of your 401K, or other retirement account to pay your living expenses. You pull money from the HELOC only for property maintenance or to invest in other properties.

You need to understand the negative consequences of using your credit cards to cover expenses related to your real estate investments. Bankers are scared of borrowers that have derogatory credit and/or large outstanding balances on their credit cards. Large balances on credit cards are either indicative of poorly managed finances or that the borrowers are living beyond their income. In either case, there is a saying in the industry "nobody runs faster than a scared banker." You must have excellent credit and low outstanding balances on your credit cards. Never use your credit cards to finance your real estate activities; instead, use cash or

HELOC loans for your business expenses.

Also understand that when you pull money out of a property by refinancing the first mortgage or through the HELOC it is not a taxable event. In other words, you are not taxed on the money at the time that you pulled out the cash. You need to understand though if you sell that property at a later date, you will receive less cash at the time of sale because of the refinance. Your basis, or costs, will be based upon the original purchase price plus any capital improvements made to the property, minus any depreciation taken while you owned the property.

If you pull out any or all of the equity by refinancing, when you actually sell the property you will receive less cash at the closing because you have already pulled part of the equity out when you refinanced. Your CPA will need to calculate your gain on the sale of any property. Just remember that your gain may be much greater than the actual amount of cash received at the time of sale. Selling price minus selling expenses minus basis equals your gain or loss. If you have already pulled out all of your equity by refinancing, you could end up with a taxable gain on the sale of the property and no cash to pay income taxes on the gain.

Example

Sales Price	$400,000.00		Sales Price	$400,000.00
-Basis	$175,000.00		-Existing Mtgs.	$320,000.00
Taxable Gain	$225,000.00		Sale Proceeds	$80,000.00

In this simplified example, the seller would have a $225,000 taxable gain but would only realize $80,000 in proceeds from the sale. Why? Because he had already refinanced and pulled out most of his equity in cash at the time of refinancing the property. Substantial amounts of the sales proceeds will be needed to pay his state and federal income taxes on the taxable gain that was realized from the sale of the property. This is a very simplified example, but it is a potential trap that catches many investors off guard. Of course, you need to consult with your CPA before making any large financial decision regarding your properties.

At this time, the tax rates for property held for 12 months, or longer, are considered long term capital gains and are currently taxed at a rate of 15% of your gain. That can, of course, be changed at any time by Congress. Some investors jump through a lot of hoops trying to

IMPORTANT CONCEPTS

avoid paying any long-term capital gains. This can be accomplished with a 1031 tax-deferred exchange. However, an exchange really limits your purchase options, and you need to reinvest all of the cash proceeds to keep it a tax deferred exchange. I prefer to pay the long term capital gain tax rate and then use the remaining money in any way that I choose. I pay a much higher rate of taxes on my normal ordinary income, so 15% on my gain seems like a bargain to me. Different strokes for different folks.

If you live in a house for 2 out of 5 years, you can sell the property and not pay any Federal Income tax on the gain. Currently, a single person can net up to $250,000 tax free and a married couple up to $500,000 tax free. This can be a huge opportunity, and everyone should be aware of this. Remember when I said newer homes tend to appreciate faster than older homes? When coupled with this tax break, appreciation creates a wonderful investment. Think about it for a while. Get your calculator out and see what kind of opportunities you may be able to create, tax free.

QUICK REVIEW

1. Anyone can make money in a "Hot Market," but you need to be able to make money and survive in a "Slow Market."
2. You must always have available adequate liquid reserves for business expenses and to survive the market swings.
3. You should have a HELOC on each property to cover expenses as they occur, and they will occur.
4. Each property should support itself financially.
5. Do not use the cash flow from one property to support the loss on another property.
6. The worst mistake you can make is to pull equity out of your property to pay off credit cards, cars, boats or vacations. This will destroy your investment program.
7. Take advantage of long term capital gains; I normally do not sell investment properties until I have owned them for at least 12 months and owner-occupied properties for twenty four months.

Do not wait for ideal circumstances, nor for the best opportunities; they will never come.

– JANET ERSKINE STUART

INSIGHT 9

Two Big Common Mistakes that Investors Make.

1. Investors build up some decent equity in their properties. and then they start burning through their equity by refinancing with "cash-out loans" and spending the money on things that have nothing to do with their investments. They act as if their properties are giant ATM machines from which they can pull free money whenever they need additional cash. If you are carrying large balances on your credit cards and pulling cash out of your investments, you are simply spending more money than you are earning. Wake up, and realize that you cannot continue in that direction without eating up the equity in your house and destroying your investment program.
2. Some investors do not maintain long term adequate cash reserves. Sooner or later, they are going to need to put cash back into their properties, either because of repairs or to cover house payments when the properties are vacant. Nothing is more important to the safety of your investment program than having adequate cash reserves and a HELOC loan on each property.

Security depends not so much upon how much you have, as upon how much you can do without.

– JOSEPH WOOD KRUTCH

IMPORTANT CONCEPTS

INSIGHT 10

If Something Can Go Wrong, It Probably Will. Plan For It.

When contemplating purchasing investment property, try to be aware of things that may create problems for you in the near future. I am not saying become a worrywart, just be realistic about possible problems that may come up. Develop a game plan to deal with potential problems, so that you will not be caught off guard if they should occur.

For instance, assume that you are thinking about purchasing a rental property. What will you need after the close of escrow? Paint, brushes, drop cloths, plumbing repairs, and landscaping might all be necessary. One item that you will definitely want as soon as possible is a good, qualified tenant. How are you going to find one? When do you start looking? What type of lease do you want to use? How much rent should you ask for? How much for security and pet deposits? These are all important questions that you will need answers to before you make an offer to purchase, not after you already own the property.

Luck is a matter of preparation meeting opportunity.

- ANON

Your experienced REALTOR® and loan officer should be able to assist you in obtaining accurate information. Remember if you are buying investment property you want a team that has experience with rental properties. This is just part of the reason why you need to deal with experienced professionals. They can save you time, headaches, money and questionable decisions. Take a piece of paper and write down everything that you can think of that you may have a question or concern about.

Perhaps you are not comfortable with the amount of cash reserves that you may or may not have available to you. Lack of cash reserves is an extremely important concern that must be addressed, even before going out and looking at properties. Perhaps your loan officer can suggest different types of loan products that will minimize the amount of up front cash that you will need for a down payment.

You may be able to structure an offer to purchase where the seller agrees to pay all or part of your closing costs. This would minimize the amount of cash needed at closing. Creative ideas require close coordination between you the buyer, your REALTOR®, and your loan officer. Everything must come together correctly at the closing, or there may not be a closing.

You want accurate information up front. It will greatly reduce the probability of future problems, and you certainly don't want inaccurate information. I have dealt with many investors that were told up front that a property would rent for $xxxxx, but found out after the close of escrow the property would only rent for substantially less than what they were originally told. This type of misleading information can hurt you financially for years. You need accurate information so that you can make good informed decisions.

We will cover how to verify information in later sections of the material. It is important to have a team working for you that you can depend on for reliable information. It is also important to discuss with them any concerns that you may have, so that they can provide you with the pertinent answers. Knowledge is powerful if you use it. You need as much accurate knowledge as possible up front.

Problems can normally be solved. However, the solutions normally require the expenditures of time and cash. These are two things that you want to try to conserve. You can minimize potential problems by allowing for them and planning ahead. Do not stick your head into the sand and hope that they will just disappear. They will not.

The difficulties and struggles of today are but the price we must pay for the accomplishments and victories of tomorrow.

- WILLIAM J.H. BOETCKER

IMPORTANT CONCEPTS

QUICK REVIEW

1. If something can go wrong, it probably will. Be prepared for the unexpected because it will happen, sooner or later. That is a big part of life, and you must be able to adapt.
2. Get accurate information up front. Do not guess or assume that you know the answers.
3. Work with experienced REALTORS® and loan officers who own rental properties.
4. Knowledge is a powerful tool. Use it to your advantage.

INSIGHT 11

"Fool's Gold" Buying or Selling as the Yield Curve is Rising.

It is not a wise decision to either buy or try to sell real estate when the yield curve is dramatically increasing. Rates typically climb for about two years and stay at their peak for about six to twelve months. When the rates are high, the market really slows down to a crawl. The property values normally do not drop substantially, but the number of houses selling decline dramatically.

Many sellers will hold on as long as possible before financial reality finally sets in and when it does there are some terrific buys. I have found, however, that if you wait until the peak period for interest rates has passed, you can find even more motivated sellers. They have been reading the newspapers for months about the collapsing real estate market and they are getting very nervous and down-right desperate to sell. Once the rates have peaked I do not start buying again until the Yield Curve has definitely started to invert.

Many investors will find a property on which the seller has lowered the price a few thousand dollars, causing the investor to get giddy and jump on the property. Thinking that the market is going to immediately rebound, the investor buys, only to find that the market continues down because rates are still too high. If the investor is planning on holding for the long term, he will eventually be fine. If he is buying to fix it up and/or just to flip it fast, he is going to have a serious financial problem on his hands. The property is not going to go away quickly in a high interest rate environment. If a property owner must sell for any reason while interest rates are high, he is facing a very expensive and frustrating experience. When interest rates are high, what appears to be a great buy may only be "Fools Gold," awaiting the inexperienced investor.

While rates are high, an investor needs to concentrate on accumulating as much cash as possible. When the market moves to its next phase the investor must be able to move quickly. There will be some very exciting opportunities for those who can recognize the timing and are prepared to take advantage of the market.

QUICK REVIEW

1. As interest rates increase, the number of property sales will decrease.
2. After interest rates have started to decline, it is a great time to start buying property.
3. It is very dangerous to buy during market peaks.

INSIGHT 12

"Real Gold" Buying or Selling as Interest Rates are Declining.

Once interest rates have peaked and the yield curve is declining, there will be some really golden opportunities for the investor who has been patiently waiting for the interest rates to peak and start declining. If you scratch and dig around, you will be able to find some true "Golden Nuggets" or "Diamonds in the Rough". I have found that I can pick up $50,000.00 to $100,000.00 in instant equity per transaction in this type of market (20 to 25% of property value).

"Golden Nuggets" are properties that are in excellent condition, are usually vacant and have been sitting on the market for several months. Please note that the seller must have a lot of equity in the property. The sellers want an "offer to buy" and their priority is moving the property. They want out. Their biggest concern is how quickly can you close the escrow? The seller may be a homeowner, investor or a bank. Bank owned property is called REO property (Real Estate Owned).

I will be able to assure them that I can move very quickly because I will have my finances in order. I do not offer them market value, and I will not purchase the property unless I am picking up a great amount of equity in the transaction. The Golden Nugget is immediately ready to be rented to a qualified tenant. There should be several qualified families available since interest rates have been high, and investors have not been buying investment properties.

"Diamonds in the Rough" will need some repairs before they can be rented. You should be prepared to move as quickly as possible in getting the repairs done. There should be qualified labor and materials available, since the market will have been slow for several months. I have even had contractors virtually beg me to give them the job because they have been out of work for an extended period of time. You can really make some unbelievable buys with "Diamonds in the Rough," but you must be ready to take advantage of the opportunities and move quickly on them.

If you have planned ahead and bought properties in areas which will be in demand, the market is going to become red-hot for sales at the end of the declining interest rate cycle.

Many buyers put off buying houses as long as rates are declining, thinking that they do not want to buy before interest rates have bottomed out. What happens in the real world is that the rates are at the bottom for just a few hours and then start increasing significantly. The buyers who have delayed suddenly come rushing into the market hoping to get locked in at the lower rates. They wind up paying more for the property and closing at a significant higher interest rate than if they had bought several months earlier.

The Changing of the Guard

When the previous Chairmen of the Federal Reserve Bank, Paul Volcker and Allen Greenspan, decided to retire, each one of them announced their retirement several months in advance of their actual retirement date. Then they both immediately started raising interest rates. They were setting the table for the next new chairman when he came into office. They raised the rates to slow down the economy, and then let the new chairman decide when to start lowering the rates. This way the new chairman could demonstrate to the world that he was going to be serious about controlling inflation and that the dollar would remain a strong currency in world affairs.

The Perfect Storm – The Last Quarter of 2006

Increases in interest rates have a huge effect on the real estate market. We know that a war will affect interest rates, and we know that different seasons of the year will affect the real estate market. If you add in 5 years of extreme appreciation in housing, the introduction of a new Fed chairman and if you throw in mid-term elections, you have created a situation for the "Perfect Storm in Real Estate". That is exactly what we experienced in the last quarter of 2006 and the market absorbed the full impact of the storm.

Hopefully, you were not trying to sell any real estate during the last quarter of 2006 and all of 2007. If so, you probably were not happy with the outcome. This is the type of market that you must try to avoid selling in at all costs. Simply stay on the sidelines and wait for the dust to clear. There will be many opportunities to make great buys and interest rates will be declining in the near future.

It is important to note some things about the market downturns which are easy to miss in all of the newspaper headlines about a collapsing real estate market. There is a small amount of decline that actually happens to the sales prices of the homes. When there is a drop in prices nearly all of it will be in the single digits, over the entire U.S. In fact, some areas will not have a market decline. A few areas will actually have appreciation during a downturn. That is nearly always the situation. Housing does not take a huge drop in price except in some seriously depressed markets that have high unemployment (Houston and Detroit are good examples).

When housing takes a big drop in price, it is because of a serious loss of jobs in the local community, not because of swings in the market. Housing slowdown is actually a slowing down of the numbers of houses sold. It is not a big decline in the price of the houses sold. The houses which do take a big drop in price are the ones sitting vacant for several months with sellers who are desperate to get out from under the payment.

New home builders are desperate to get rid of their inventory for the same reasons. They are sitting on hundreds of millions of dollars of inventory that they need to move. A new home builder cannot simply decide to suspend sales for a few months. They must move the inventory because more houses are already in the pipeline. It takes several years for a builder to buy land, develop it, build it out and market the final product.

IMPORTANT CONCEPTS

I usually begin looking for potential purchases in the market place during the first quarter of the year. I am never in a hurry because there will always be available properties. Remember the winter months are the slow months for sales, and inventories build up. I like to start looking at new homes and vacant re-sales which have been sitting on the market for several months. In other words, I like to know that I am dealing with motivated sellers who want out. I am not afraid of hurting someone's feelings or of having my offer rejected. As an investor I want to buy equity that can be converted to cash at a later date.

If I find a property on which I am interested in making an offer, I usually work with a local real estate agent that I trust and with whom I have a good working relationship. In turn, when I have a client who needs an experienced real estate broker, I know several who will do an excellent job. These are very conscientious agents who wish to do business with me and my customers in the future. It works out well for everyone involved in the relationship. This is the type of team you should have working for you in your real estate program, either as an investor, or as a homeowner.

QUICK REVIEW

1. As interest rates start to decline, start buying property. Do not wait for the bottom of the interest rate cycle.
2. Look for properties with immediate equity. Do not pay full market value.
3. Fix-up properties may be "Diamonds in the Rough," but you always want at least 30% equity in the property at the time of purchase.
4. As an investor I want to buy equity that can be converted to cash at a later date.

INSIGHT 13

You Can Make Money in a Slow Market as Well as a Hot Market.

You actually make more money from real estate in a slow market than during a fast moving market. It is much easier to make great buys in a slow market because you're dealing with motivated sellers who need to sell. It is just like the stock market. Investors can make good returns when they are getting 20% on their stock portfolios and may even earn hundreds of thousands of dollars on their investments. However, the people that start buying right after a major market correction can make millions on their investments. They are buying when everyone else is selling. They are getting fantastic buys from very motivated sellers.

When the stock market makes a huge market adjustment down in value, have the companies that you own stock in suddenly collapsed over night? Have they suddenly lost all of their business? Have their cash assets suddenly disappeared? Have their products that they have been making for the last 30 to 100 years suddenly become worthless? Of course not, they are still conducting business as usual. Nothing has happened to the company or to its markets. The value of its stock dropped on the open markets, but it is still the same company, with the same products or providing the same services with the same employees. By the way, have you ever noticed that when the stock market declines it is called a "market correction," versus a "market downturn or decline," for real estate?

It is the same with our nation's supply of housing. Prices may increase, stay the same or decrease, but the housing is not going to become worthless. We have 300 million people who need a place to live and work. That demand will not disappear just because of fluctuations in the market. In fact, it is growing at a very fast pace as our population increases.

The last new house built should be the most expensive house on the market, compared to similar houses. The price of land, material and labor continue to increase over time, thus pushing up the price of housing, faster than the rate of inflation.

I normally do not buy houses while sales are declining (interest rates are at their peak). I wait until I am certain that rates have peaked and have started to decline. Then I look for houses which are vacant and have been sitting on the market for several months. I make low offers and find out just exactly how motivated the seller really is.

I do not like closing escrow in the months from October through January unless the seller is willing to "rent back" from me until the first of February. It is very difficult to rent a house during the holidays, and I don't want to be bothered trying to rent a house during those months. If I use a good property manager it may not be so bad; however, I believe any property manager will find it very difficult to rent property during that time period. Vacant houses can cost the landlord a lot of money at an expensive time of the year. You really do not want to travel down that road during the holiday months if you can avoid it.

After the rates have declined and the housing market has not yet fully recovered from a market slump, I like to start shopping. Yes, I will be paying a fairly high interest rate at the time, however I will be getting a great buy on the property (or I do not buy). Remember as an investor you want to buy immediate equity in the property. Then I will plan on refinancing the property at a later date and at a lower interest rate.

If you think of real estate as a long term investment it always goes up over the long haul. Have you ever heard of a house going down in value over a 5, 10 or 20 year time period? It can happen, but it usually is because of an extreme negative change in the local economy.

You only need one good buy per year.

Remember as rates drop, property values will increase. I may be able to refinance at a lower rate and do a "cash-out refinance", and get most or all of my original cash investment back. The property should have increased in value, and I should have bought it below market value at the time of purchase. If everything works out correctly, I should be able to refinance in a few months, get all or most of my money back out of the property, and lower my monthly payment because of lower interest rates.

I do not take out a thirty year loan with any intention of keeping that loan for thirty years. There will be too many opportunities to refinance and take out some of the equity. I will use that equity to purchase other properties. I do not want a lot of equity sitting in a house because it is not earning anything while it is tied up in the property. You cannot buy groceries with equity, and it does not earn interest. At the same time, do not pull out all of your equity in a property, I try to keep a least 30% equity. That means that whatever the value of the property, I have at least 30% of that value remaining in equity.

When I am thinking about selling a house, I assume that it is going to cost me about 10% of the value of the property for selling expenses. That includes normal selling costs plus 6% commission, plus repairs and the vacancy factor. If you refinance a property at 100% of its value, you may need to come up with about 10% of its value in cash to cover your selling costs. That could be a financial disaster for many families. That's why I never recommend refinancing your properties to over 70% of their value. With one-hundred percent financing you could be creating a huge financial risk that you should not take.

Remember, if your property has appreciated in value, and you pulled out cash and then decide to sell, you may have a substantial capital gains or income tax obligation. Please consult your tax advisor before selling or refinancing any property as it may save you a lot of money in both state and federal taxes.

QUICK REVIEW

1. Housing is always going to maintain its value over time. The U.S. has a fast-growing population, and everyone needs a place to live.
2. As interest rates decline property values will increase.

INSIGHT 14

It is Best to Buy into a Soft Market and Sell into a Strong Market.

We live in a capitalistic economy. In this type of economy it is acceptable to make money from other people's poor planning. You are not responsible for their losses, but you may profit from their losses. If you don't, someone else will. I am a capitalist, and proud of it. I am also aware that if I mess up someone is going to make money from my mistakes. A free enterprise economy can be very efficient. It will reward efficiency and it will punish the inefficient. It can be a beautiful machine, but it has no mercy and can be extremely brutal to those who do not plan well and execute their plans wisely.

IMPORTANT CONCEPTS

When I pick-up a newspaper and read about the "gloom and doom" in the real estate market I can't control myself—I am smiling from ear to ear. You should understand that most *investigative* newspaper reporters do not know anything about the real estate markets. Their job is to make headlines and sell newspapers. They will tell you that they have the resources to make contact with experts in the various industries, which is true. However, are they contacting the correct so-called experts? And better yet, are they reporting what the experts actually told them, or are they distorting the information to suit their own purpose? Shock, disbelief and fear sells newspapers; not responsible news reporting.

I have found that most *real estate* reporters do a much better job of conveying an accurate picture of the real estate markets. In Phoenix, I have noticed that the investigative reporters always like to contact specific real estate brokers about what is happening in the market. I have known these brokers for years and I know that most of them have never owned investment properties. In fact, the National Association of REALTORS® says that only about 4% of all REALTORS® own investment properties. REALTORS® are salespeople and if you ask them if they own investment properties most of them will tell you "no, I just don't have the time to invest in real estate." Selling is how they make a living. They do not make the time to invest in the very product they sell.

It is easy to pick up several thousand or tens of thousands of dollars of immediate equity in a soft market. Just remember if you try to immediately resell the property in that same soft market, you may just be taking the place of the previous owner. If you are buying in a soft market, you must plan on holding onto the property at least until the market has improved (interest rates have declined).

In a soft market, there is a shortage of buyers and a surplus of sellers. Nervous sellers will sell their properties substantially below market values. You can buy excellent properties for 20% to 25% below market value; start by looking at vacant homes that have been on the market for 60 days, or more. You will probably be dealing with a motivated seller. The seller needs to have a lot of equity in the property. Learn if they have owned it for several years. If so, they should have substantial equity.

Personally, I never could see the point in buying and then immediately reselling a property. If you choose to do so, the gain is taxed as ordinary income. That means that you put in your time, effort, and cash and assumed all risks and then split the profit (if any) with the federal and state governments. I prefer to hold onto the property for at least a year, at which time I am paying on the basis of long term capital gains, rather than ordinary income. Currently, long-term capital gains are taxed at a lower rate than ordinary income. If your ordinary income is not very high, it may make sense to you to go ahead and pay taxes on the gain as ordinary income.

It is very difficult psychologically for a lot of investors to sell their property in a strong market. They are afraid the property will continue to appreciate after they have sold it to another party. If you do not have plans or need to sell any property for several years, my advice is do not sell. Hold onto the property, as long as it continues to be a solid investment.

If you are planning on selling in the near future don't try to time the market just so that you may receive the highest price. That is very difficult to do and more than likely it will not happen as you planned. Sell the property while the market is strong, because you can get an excellent price, a good buyer and minimize your marketing time. Do not blow a strong market; take advantage of it.

If a market is excessively strong, do not try to buy real estate. Wait for it to calm down. It will happen sooner than you think. In 2005, the market in Phoenix, AZ was extremely strong and properties were selling in a matter of a few days with several offers to purchase from different buyers. This is the optimum market in which to be selling, but not buying. Property was appreciating at about 50% per annum, and buyers were desperate. This simply was not a healthy market.

The new home market was completely insane, and the new home builders were doing everything they could to keep investors out of the markets. Not only did they keep the investors out of the market, they soon became extremely arrogant as to how they treated regular owner-occupied home buyers. They increased the required deposits to $25,000 per sales contract, and the deposits were non-refundable. If you could not close escrow for any reason, you lost your deposit. It was so bad, that they were holding lotteries at the subdivisions to see who would be next in line to be able to buy one of their houses.

Towards the end of the market cycle, I was entering into a contract to purchase a new home I was going to owner occupy. I thought I had completed the entire contract and gave the builder's sales clerk a check for $25,000, and as I was leaving the sales office, she suddenly called me back. She said that she had a new addendum that I had to sign and date. It had absolutely no significance and she had forgotten all about it, until I was walking out. The addendum was very short and to the point. It said that the builder had the right at any time and for any reason, to record a $40,000 second lien against the property during the first 12 months after the close of escrow.

I asked what that was for and she replied that the builders were all going to require that addendum on any new home being built in the state. She informed me that I would never be able to buy a new home again in the state without signing that addendum. I was not only very irritated with her for waiting until the very end of the contract to explain about the "insignificant addendum," but I also thought that it was the height of arrogance on the builder's part.

I informed her that there was absolutely no chance I was going to sign it. I also told her the new home builders were very close to a major "attitude adjustment," because of market changes that were right around the corner. Of course, she did not have any idea of what I was talking about. However, just a few months later she found out. In that time period, the market had completely turned around for the worse; especially for the new home builders.

I happened to be driving by that same subdivision, so I decided to stop in and see how they were doing. That same house, on the same lot, in the same subdivision, was still very much for sale nearly a year after I had tried to purchase it. I asked if they still required that $40,000 addendum to the purchase contract and they said "no", that silly thing went away.

Never fall into the trap of believing that the market can only continue in one direction, up or down. It never has, and it never will. If you find yourself in a market that is extremely strong, do not hesitate to walk away from a purchase. The market will adjust back to a more normal market situation, and when it adjusts, it will not be a pretty sight for a lot of property owners who paid too much for their property. I am probably fortunate that I did not buy the property. I owned other properties in the immediate area and thought it would be a good location for me, even though I was well aware that a market correction was coming.

It is a much safer investment to buy property when the market is soft and sellers are extremely motivated to sell. You can purchase properties in a soft market and very realistically start out with 15% to 25% equity in the property.

Your best buys will be made in a soft market.

If you are thinking of purchasing a new home, there are a few key items to always keep in mind. You will probably be paying full market value at the time of purchase for any new home. New homes are appraised differently than re-sales. New homes are appraised based on the "costs to build," while re-sales are appraised on "comparable sales" in the immediate area.

The other thing that is important to know about new homes is that you will need to invest substantial amounts of additional funds in a new home after you own it, to make it livable. New homes normally do not come with landscaping, window coverings and ceiling fans. When you purchase a new home you are betting that the house will appreciate enough in the future to make it a good investment. That may or may not be the case, depending upon current interest rates and new job creation in the area.

QUICK REVIEW

1. You will get a better buy in a soft market, new or existing, and you can pick up immediate equity in a property.
2. It is best to sell into a strong market. You will receive a good price, deal with motivated buyers, and experience minimum selling time. In a very strong market, the buyers are very hesitant to ask for changes to the property or to have the seller help with their buying expenses.
3. It is psychologically very hard for most people to sell their property in a strong market. They tend to hold on too long and the market can change for the worse very quickly.
4. Long-term capital gains are taxed at lower rates than ordinary income.
5. When purchasing a new home, you will be paying market value for the property. The sales price of a new home is established by the "costs to build," not by comparable sales of similar properties.

INSIGHT 15

Look at Recent "Comparable Sales" and Recent "Comparable Rents" Before Buying.

Always look carefully at "comparable sales" before making an offer to purchase a property. You absolutely need to know what similar properties have sold for in the last six months. Similar properties are houses in the same neighborhood or the same sub-division. They should be within 10% (plus or minus) of the same livable square footage and approximately the same age. If one house has an in-ground pool, or other similar amenities, and the other does not, you will need to adjust the values accordingly. You should to talk to a REALTOR® or appraiser to see how much an in ground pool would affect the prices in the area.

It is not difficult to become accurate with your evaluations with a little practice. You may want to drive by your comparables and see how their appearance compares to your subject property. It is extremely important to do your homework. It is not difficult, and could save you from making a major mistake or missing out on a golden opportunity.

If you are using a realty company, they should be able to run the comparable sales from the Multiple Listing Service for your subject property, and then you can drive by and check each property out. Look at the neighborhood, the amenities of the area and the location of the subject property. Is it close to a busy street or does it back up to a shopping center? Maybe it's across the street from a beautiful park. Location is extremely important. Always remember that some day you will want to sell that property. *The time to start thinking about selling is before you purchase, not after you own the property.*

Location is one of the most important features for any residential property. It is also the one feature that you cannot change. Floor plans can be changed, the number of bedrooms can be changed, the square footage can change, colors are very easy to change, but location does not change. If a house is facing a "somewhat busy street," in a few years it may be facing an expressway, or even a freeway. I try to buy property on the interior of a subdivision for that reason. I want to have a minimum amount of noise and traffic, inside and outside, of a property.

Never pay more for a property than the comparable sales indicate it is worth. There are too many properties for sale to justify paying more than market value for a house. I seldom pay full market value when I purchase a property. I want immediate equity, or I simply do not buy. If I cannot buy a property below market value I will simply wait until the market gets a little softer, which nearly always happens towards the end of the year or the beginning of the next year. Take your time. This is a business, run it like a business. *There are times of the year that are better to buy, just like there are better times of the year to be selling.*

There are markets that are better to buy in and markets that are better to sell in. That's life. Take advantage of market conditions and do not fight the Fed.

Never purchase investment property without thoroughly checking out the market rents for the property. It is just as important as checking out the comparable sales and can be done at the same time. I do not have any idea of how many times I have had new investors come to me for investor financing on a property that they had just purchased thinking that it would rent for a certain dollar amount per month. After we did our research or received the appraisal, we would discover that the market rent was substantially less than the new investor had originally been told. An experienced investor will not make this mistake.

You do not want to sign a purchase contract without knowing what market rents are for the property. You do not want to learn you must subsidize the property each month for several years unless you're just looking for a tax write off. That reminds me, I do not ever recommend purchasing real estate just because you think that you need a tax deduction. That is like spending a dollar to get a $.40 tax deduction. You would be better off just donating the money to a tax deductible cause.

Rents are easy to determine. Just look in the newspaper for similar properties in the same area. Your REALTOR® can give you a print out of all the properties that have rented through the Multiple Listing Services in that immediate area for the last six months. You may also want to check out some on-line services that are available, usually for free.

One on-line service that is very interesting is **www.craigslist.com**. You can look at property for sale or for rent in just about any major city in the world. There is an incredible amount of information on the website, but the real estate sections are the most interesting. You can look at property literally just about anywhere in the world, Germany, England, Finland, South America, Canada, and etc. Once you start looking at prices around the world you quickly realize that prices in the U.S. look like a real bargain in comparison.

If you think education is expensive, try ignorance.

- DEREK BOK

IMPORTANT CONCEPTS

QUICK REVIEW

1. Always check out similar comparable sales before buying.
2. The time to think about selling is before making the purchase, not after you own the property.
3. Location of the property should work for you, not against you.
4. Investing is a business and should be run as a business.
5. Always check out the comparable rents before buying an investment property.

INSIGHT 16

Take Your Time Before Buying: "Fools Rush in Where Angels Fear to Tread."

Never let your emotions take control of your buying decisions. Buying is a very emotional process and you must learn to control your emotions. Learn to recognize when you are thinking from an emotional viewpoint, rather than thinking logically. Remember, this is a huge business decision, whether you are a first time home buyer or a seasoned investor. *Buying a house is a business decision and should be approached as a business decision.*

Take your time and do not let anyone rush you into a decision. If you think you have found the "perfect house," you are absolutely wrong. There is no such thing as the "perfect house" any more than there is a "perfect automobile." Always think about the property, at least overnight. It is simply too large a decision to rush. If the property sells there will always be more houses for sale. This country is not going to run out of houses for sale. What may seem like the perfect house at the time will definitely have some drawbacks that will become apparent after careful evaluation.

I would recommend that any buyer look at least twelve to fourteen houses before trying to make a purchase decision. If you take your time and carefully evaluate each house, you will be able to make a wise and informed decision. As you are looking at houses, be sure and take detailed notes and photographs of each property as you're previewing them, otherwise you will be confused as to which house had which features.

As you are previewing, try to decide which features are the most important to you and your family. It is very common for most families not to know what is important to them until they start looking. You and your spouse need to discuss each feature and how important they are to each of you. Hopefully both of you can come to an agreement on what is important and what is not.

Buying a house can be a very stressful process for most people. It is a process that deserves time, communication and patience. Like anything, the more that you do it, the easier it becomes. As an investor, it does not take me long to decide if I am interested in a property. It becomes similar to deciding where I am going for lunch or dinner that day. Emotions are not a large part of that decision process, but admittedly I do not need to be concerned about as many things as an average family must consider. Just remember to make a patient, logical decision, and not one based on raging emotions. A real estate auction can be a very dangerous situation in which to buy a property because emotions tend to run very high at an auction, where an immediate on-the-spot decision is required.

Always remember, anyone can buy a house. That's the easy part. You must remember to buy a house that will be easy to sell in the future. *It is far more important to be able to sell than it is to be able to buy a property.* If you need to sell, you probably need to sell now, and it may not be a decent market at the time. Always consider the salability of a property before purchasing. *Remember, the selling process begins with the purchase.*

> *The haves and the have-nots can often be traced back to the dids and the did-nots.*
>
> - D. O. FLYNN

IMPORTANT CONCEPTS

QUICK REVIEW

1. Most people make emotional decisions when buying. Try to make logical buying decisions.
2. There is no such thing as the perfect home.
3. It is far more important to be able to sell than it is to be able to buy. The selling process begins with the selection of a property at the time of purchase.

CHAPTER FOUR

THE MAGIC OF THE INTERNET

INSIGHT 17

Utilizing the Internet with Real Estate Investments

One of the most important sources of current real estate information can be found on your local Multiple Listing Services. Most people will not have immediate access to the MLS. However it is available by logging on to **www.Realtor.com**. This will give information on property currently listed for sale on the MLS all over the U.S. If you use a REALTOR® when purchasing property, that REALTOR® should be glad to provide you with whatever additional information that you may need.

However, there are some wonderful websites that you can access on your own. Your REALTOR® may not even know they exist. The first one I would like to refer you to is **www.mgic.com/mkttrend.html**, which is published by MGIC, a mortgage insurance company. A mortgage insurance company insures the loan amount which exceeds 80% of the Loan to Value (LTV).

Since MGIC is insuring the top portion of the loan, they spend a great deal of money analyzing the various real estate markets around the country. They do a wonderful job explaining how the various markets are being affected by local market forces. You can pull up just about any major market in the country. It is really interesting to see how the various markets are performing. At any one time there may be markets showing tremendous growth and appreciation, while at the same time there may be cities that are really hurting.

I really appreciate MGIC placing this information on the web. I use it often and I find it to be an extremely helpful source of information. *You should notice a couple things they always comment about are job growth and income growth. These are an indication of how important those two factors are in analyzing local real estate markets.*

A similar web site is published by Private Mortgage Group, which is also a mortgage insurance company. Their website is **www.pmigroup.com**, and they take a different approach to explaining the markets. They often provide interesting commentaries on their website. This is extremely valuable information, and I very much appreciate the company making it available.

I previously mentioned **www.craigslist.com**, which does an excellent job of letting you see what is on the market either for rent or for sale all over the world.

A great free newsletter located at **perspectives@globalinsight.com** provides quarterly valuations on house prices in most of the major cities. It does a good job of breaking down the various markets in relation to being "overvalued or undervalued." The valuation ratings are based on several criteria including house prices, interest rates, household incomes and population densities. They show the current rate of appreciation in various parts of the country, a great valuation summary chart and metropolitan area house valuations rankings. You must study the material to fully understand what they are providing to their readers. This is important information you should utilize in your investment program.

You can study the material and very quickly determine which part of the country is overvalued and which part is undervalued, and by how much. I think that you will find it very interesting and informative reading.

Great Web Sites for Economic Indicators

As mentioned previously, the yield curve is the most accurate indicator for future economic activity. It is not created by the government or any private party, but comes from the financial markets. It indicates where professional investors think the economy is headed. The yield curve can be located at **www.ustreas.gov/offices/domestic-finance/debt-management/interest-rate/yield.shtml**. This is one of the U.S. Treasury web sites (only the government would have an address that goes on forever).

When the yield curve is curving up, investors expect inflation to be increasing. If the yield curve is flat, the economy will be slowing down and may be headed for a recession. Should the yield curve be curving down, we are more than likely headed into a recession. *This leading indicator should be a real estate investor's primary indicator of the direction of the economy.*

The Consumer Price Index (CPI) is the best indicator of price inflation for goods and services. Inflation has an affect on everyone as it determines how much the price of goods and services is increasing. As inflation increases, it forces businesses to raise prices to cover their additional costs of conducting business. Labor will want salary increases that will cover the additional costs that workers must pay for goods and services. Families on fixed incomes can be hurt the most as inflation increases and prices rise.

Real estate usually increases in value slightly faster than the rate of inflation. As materials, land and labor increase in price, it increases the value of existing residential properties. Real estate is a good investment because it serves as a hedge against inflation. However, be aware that if inflation exceeds 2% the Feds are going to dramatically raise interest rates. This will hit the real estate market extremely hard and home values will tend to decline.

A website which will give you far more information than you ever wanted to know about inflation is **www.bls.gov/cpi/**. You can create your own spreadsheets with information about inflation from 1913 to the latest released information. You can also break it down into regions of the country and even individual cities. If you are into spreadsheets and want to know about inflation, this website was made for you.

Existing home sales are important because eight out of ten homes sold are re-sales. An increase in home sales indicates that families are feeling good about their employment and financial situation. During a recession, home sales are one of the leading indicators that the worst of the recession is over, and it is a big factor in pulling the economy out of a recession. New homes have a larger impact upon the economy than re-sales. Re-sales only involve transferring title from a current owner to the next owner, while new home sales require construction of the new house. This construction process creates new jobs in the economy.

I like the following address: **www.realtor.org**. It provides up-to-date information on several housing indicators such as existing home sales, pending home sales, housing affordability and one of my favorites, mortgage applications. It is really good information that is both helpful and accurate. It also provides current information on important economic indicators such as CPI, GDP, Employment Situation and Consumer Confidence. This is provided because the organization obviously believes it is important information for the real estate industry.

You can try **www.bankrate.com**, a good website to view current interest rates on everything from credit cards, automobiles, mortgages and home equity lines of credit. The website provides a wealth of information that will give you an idea of current market rates.

I would caution everyone to think twice about giving out your personal financial information over the web. I have had dozens of borrowers come to me for help after they had given out their financial information and learned it had been sold 100's of times to various lenders and organizations. This is what the mortgage industry refers to as selling leads. I call it handing over your financial information on a silver tray. It may reach the point that the investor must change phone numbers and pay a company to monitor credit reports for unusual activity and simply hope for the best. At the very least, check out the company's "privacy policy" before giving out any personal or financial information.

The Bureau of Economic Analysis, run by the U.S. Dept. of Commerce, operates **www.bea.gov**. They produce information about balance of trade, gross domestic product, and personal income.

www.bls.gov is operated by the Bureau of Labor Statistics and provides information regarding employment, income, consumer price index, and wages and spending. You can get a breakdown by region, state and local areas.

www.fanniemae.com and **www.freddiemac.com** both provide monthly market outlooks on the real estate markets. I find their comments very useful.

www.mbaa.org. The Mortgage Bankers Association produces housing and mortgage reports, news reports, and economic forecasts.

www.nahb.org. The National Association of Home Builders provides all kinds of information about new home markets, products, industry news, and other various reports.

ADDITIONAL INFORMATIVE WEB SITES

Aerial Photos

www.earth.google.com Aerial views of anywhere in the world. They have a free version and a 3-D version that currently costs $400.00 per year. They have done amazing things with satellite photos.

Business and economic news

www.forbes.com Great for financial news.
www.money.com General financial news.
www.yahoo.com Great for current financial news.

Foreclosures

www.foreclosures.com Lists all kinds of items of government foreclosures including real estate.
www.all-foreclosure.com Lists government and bank foreclosures.

Interest Rate Graphs

www.mortgage-x.com/library/loans.htm This site has a tremendous number of interest rate graphs. It also has a calculator where you can pick a starting date and compare the different indices and see which one would give a better interest rate in different types of markets. I like to play with this calculator when I have time.

Landlord Information

www.mrlandlord.com Much information for landlords including rental forms and landlord/tenant laws in all states.
www.rentlaw.com Sample contracts, leases and all types of contracts and agreements.

Property Values

www.zillow.com Is a great site for estimating the value of any property that you may want to check out. You can also post a property for sale on the site.
www.realestate.yahoo.com This site will show you all of the current comparable sales for a property by date and square footage. Well worth checking out if you need to know the value of homes in an area.

Rental Sites

www.craigslist.com Rental and sales information on properties around the world.
www.forrent.com Nice layout for rental homes across the country.
www.rentals.com Rental properties by cities in the U.S.

Reverse Mortgages

www.financialfreedom.com. Compare the three reverse mortgages by using the reverse mortgage calculator.

Legal Web Sites

www.legalzoom.com. Various legal information including creating your own legal trusts, partnerships, and corporations, plus much more legal information.

On-Line Banks

www.emigrantdirect.com An on-line bank that is FDIC insured and is currently paying 5% interest on savings account. No minimum deposit is required. The savings account is tied to your current checking account that enables you to transfer money from your checking into their savings account.

www.ingdirect.com Same as above. I have accounts with both banks and I have been very satisfied with both of them. Check them out. They are huge banking institutions and the accounts are FDIC insured.

The above internet sites provide extremely valuable information to a potential homeowner or investor, and most of the information is free for the using. Due to the availability of reliable information, I believe it is becoming easier to be a success at real estate investing than in the past. The Fed is doing a much better job of controlling the economy and inflation, money is cheaper and more abundant, and it is much easier to obtain extremely valuable information regarding the markets. This type of information simply was not readily available a few years back and the costs to obtain it would have been enormous.

The information is there for the using if you will just take the time to find it, understand it and use it. Hopefully, this book will guide you in the right direction so that you can benefit from the material. I have no doubt that there will be even more information available in the future for everyone to use. If you find any great websites out there, I would love to hear from you

CHAPTER FIVE

BUYERS PREPARATION

INSIGHT 18

Buying a Home can be Confusing and very Intimidating.

Buying a home is a huge financial decision and most buyers simply are not prepared for what is involved in the process, especially first time homebuyers. The very first step is to get a current copy of your credit report and find out what kind of information is being reported on it. Many first-time homebuyers have never seen a copy of their credit report and have no idea what their credit is like or what the information means.

Once you have a current copy of your credit, have someone explain exactly what the information means. Then get busy repairing your credit as needed: unpaid collections should be paid and any account that is delinquent needs to be paid current. State and Federal tax liens will need to be paid and any unpaid child support and student loans will need to be paid current.

You should have a minimum FICO score of 640 and the above items paid or paid current. If you have a score around 620, it will probably be very easy to raise the score by 40 to 70 points depending upon what is showing on the credit report. One of the most common mistakes is for a borrower to max out just one of their revolving credit accounts.

A revolving credit account is an account which allows the borrower to make a partial payment, with the balance of the billing simply "revolving" (being carried forward) without penalty to the next month. Each credit card account will be approved for a maximum amount of credit. Let's assume that your account is approved for a maximum account balance of $1,000.00. If you let the loan balance exceed 50% of the account maximum balance ($500.00), you will lower your credit score by 80 to 100 points.

At that point you have two possible ways of increasing your score. The first would be to pay the account balance down below $500.00 (1/2 of $1,000.00) or you might call the issuer of the credit card and ask them to increase your credit limit. If they agree to increase the limit to $2,000.00, or more, then you will be below 50% of your credit limit.

Please note that it can take several months to clean up a damaged credit report. This is not something that you want to ignore and hope for the best. You must be knowledgeable and take control. I run my credit report at least twice a year to see what is on it. *My credit is my most valuable asset*. It makes me money, and your excellent credit can make you money. Poor credit will cost you money in higher fees and interest rates on all financed products.

As you are working on your credit, meet with a lender and learn what type of loan would be best for you. How much cash are you going to need for down payment and closing costs? How much of a monthly payment can you qualify for, and how does that compare with the amount that you would be comfortable paying? It is easy to get borrowers qualified and approved for a much higher payment than they can handle psychologically. If, for example, you have been living at home with your parents for free, it can be frightening to suddenly take on a $1,500.00 monthly house payment. It is wise to deal with these issues in advance before going out and purchasing a home.

Work with a full time lender with experience and professional credentials who will help you find a loan type and amount which will work for you. Avoid paying discount points and getting a loan with a pre-payment penalty. Get a Good Faith Estimate and a Truth in Lending in writing. Make sure that you understand all of the loan terms and conditions. They are not very difficult to read and understand, but if there are concerns, have someone else look at the forms and explain them to you.

Get an experienced, full time REALTOR® to work for you. Take advantage of his or her experience and knowledge. It will save you time and money and keep you from making a bad financial decision. When selecting a REALTOR®, find one who will take the time to listen to what you want in a house, such as location and size. If you find that he or she is simply showing you their current listings or the current listings in their office, get a different REALTOR®. Do not waste any more time with an agent if they are not showing you the type of property that you want or need.

If you have gotten this far you have cleaned up your credit, you have found a lender you like and you have a REALTOR® who is working for you. Three items you always want when purchasing a home are a home inspection report, termite inspection and termite clearance on the property. It will cost you $300.00 to $400.00 for the inspections, but it could save you from making a horrible decision which could cost thousands of dollars in repairs. No exceptions: always get a home inspection, termite inspection and termite clearance before closing escrow on a house. It is money well spent. Ask your REALTOR® to negotiate with the seller to cover part of the inspection costs.

BUYER PREPARATION

QUICK REVIEW

1. Meet with a full time professional loan officer that has experience and credentials and have them check your credit. What is your credit like? Is it clean with a high credit score or does it need some serious repair work?
2. If your credit report needs repairs, get started. It takes time to repair credit.
3. Find out how much of a loan you can qualify for. This will determine what price homes you should be considering; never look at homes that you cannot afford.
4. How much cash do you have available and how much will be needed? Remember, you will have a down payment plus closing costs to pay.
5. Find a full time REALTOR® who will take time to find out what you want and show you that type of property. If he or she starts out just showing you their current listings, find a different REALTOR®.
6. If you decide to work with a full service broker, which is a real estate company that provides the lender and the title company, realize you will be paying a lot more for both services.
7. Preview at least 12 or 14 homes before making up your mind.
8. Take notes and photos while you are previewing the properties.
9. Never make a rushed decision. Take your time. Think about it overnight and remember that there is no such thing as a perfect property.
10. Do not feel like you have to make a full price offer for the property. It may not be worth what the seller is asking.
11. Always get a property inspection, a termite inspection and a termite clearance.
12. Read and make sure you understand all of the loan documents as well as the purchase documents. You will be signing legal documents that have legal consequences.

INSIGHT 19

Consumer Debt Versus Mortgage Debt.

As a mortgage banker, I look at consumers financial files all day long. I know what their income is, how much they have in savings, retirement, their credit and outstanding debts. It is really interesting to see how different families manage their personal finances. Let me start out by stating that it does not matter how much a family makes, what is important is how much they save or accumulate. One borrower may make hundreds of thousands of dollars per year and have terrible credit, a large burden of debt and no assets. The next borrower may have very limited income, excellent credit, no debt and a multitude of accumulated assets.

The world seems to be divided into spenders versus savers, horrible credit versus great credit, buried in debt versus very limited debt and no assets versus a lot of assets. You probably already have a good idea of how you fit into these categories. If you do not know, simply sit down with a pencil and paper and start calculating. On one side of the paper, list all of your assets and their value. On the other side, list all of your monthly and total liabilities. Then calculate the totals at the bottom of the sheet. Hopefully, the assets total substantially more than the liabilities. If they do not, maybe it is time to consider making some changes in your personal finances.

I would like to state again that my most valuable asset is my credit because it makes me money. *Your good credit can also make you money, if you use it correctly.* Let's start with borrower's credit scores. Everyone should know by now that each of us has a credit score. Those scores vary from 300 to 900; 300 to 600 is the bottom tier of the credit scores, 600 to 680 is the middle tier of the scores and 680 and higher is the top tier of borrower's scores. The higher the credit scores, the lower the interest rate the borrower will be charged for a mortgage. The lower the score, the higher the interest rate, because the risk to the lender is much greater. The borrower's income has nothing to do with his or her credit score. High income borrowers have the same percentage of high credit scores and low credit scores as low income borrowers. A score of 640 is considered the bottom score for a regular conforming mortgage when purchasing a house. A borrower can borrow money for the purchase of a house with a lower score, but the interest rate and the down payment will be higher.

As a mortgage banker, I often assist my clients with their credit repair. If I can help them increase their credit scores I can get them a lower rate of interest and better terms on their loans. Depending upon what is affecting their scores, they can sometimes increase their scores by 80 to 100 points within 30 to 40 days. This has a huge affect on the interest rate they will pay to get a new mortgage. There are licensed credit repair companies which will assist borrowers in need of serious credit repairing.

I am going to assume that you have good credit, or you probably would not be interested in this book. Your good credit can be used to increase your financial net worth or it can be used to bury yourself in consumer loans and credit cards. The choice is yours. How do you wish to spend your income and good credit?

Consumer loans include such items as credit cards, auto loans, furniture and student loans. Investment loans for this material are going to be referred to as mortgages. If you have a large amount of debt, especially credit card debt, you are simply spending more money per year than you're earning. Your outstanding credit card balance, divided by your monthly net income, tells you how many months of future income you have already spent. Such spending is actually very good for the local economy, but it is not good for your personal finances.

Credit cards carry very high rates of interest and high fees for anything the credit card company can dream up as an additional charge on your account. If you make the minimum payment and no other additional charges to that account, it will take about 18 years to pay off the balance. The problem is that people continue using the card any time that there is credit available on the account. Financially, they are on an escalator going further and further down in debt.

> *What some people mistake for the high cost of living is really the cost of living high.*
>
> - DOUG LARSON

First-time homebuyers make up about 40% of the market. They do not necessarily buy small starter homes for their first home. At the same time some elderly buyers may be trading down to smaller homes. About 80% of home sales are resale homes, and 20% are new homes. According to the National Association of REALTORS®, approximately 64% of home purchases are for primary occupancy, 23% are investment purchase and 13% are second or vacation homes.

When I am working to determine how much of a loan the borrower can qualify for there are two parts to the equation. The first part is his gross monthly income. The second part is his monthly contractual debt service he must pay out each month. As a rule of thumb, you can take the gross monthly income and multiply it by 40%. For example, $5,000 per month times 40% equals $2000.00 per month. Total monthly obligation is how much total monthly payments the borrower can qualify for per month including their new house payment. From the $2000.00, we must subtract all outstanding contractual obligations to determine how much of a house payment for which the borrower can qualify.

$5,000.00	$2,000.00 40% of Gross Income
	- 400.00 Auto
X .40	- 500.00 Credit Cards
$2,000.00 Max Qualifying Obligations	$1,100.00 Maximum Qualifying House Payment

Existing monthly debts require 2.5 times that amount in income to offset the monthly payments. It takes $1,250.00 of income to offset the $500.00 in credit card debt. For example, let's assume that the borrowers have a car loan with payments of $600.00 plus $200.00 per month in credit card debts, $800 times 2.5 equals $2000 per month. In this case the borrowers would not qualify for any additional debt. They either need to increase their income or reduce their monthly debt service.

It is very common to see applications where the borrowers have $30,000.00, $40,000.00 sometimes even $80,000.00 in outstanding credit card debts. The Federal Government now requires credit card companies to require a minimum payment of 4% each month on credit card debt. $10,000.00 times 4% equals $400.00 minimum payment per month per $10,000.00 of outstanding debt. When trying to qualify for a mortgage $400.00 per month times 2.5 equals $1,000.00 of income required each month per each $10,000.00 in outstanding credit card debts.

I see applications with $20,000 to $40,000 in outstanding credit card debts plus two car payments of $500 to $700 per month plus $100,000.00 in outstanding student loans. When I see this, I realize that I have just found a tenant looking for a nice house to rent for several years, even though they may not know it. This is a family that has decided to "live the good life now" and not be concerned about purchasing a home for several years to come. Of course, I will offer to accommodate them with a very nice rental property if they are interested.

Let's compare this family to a family with a slightly different approach to their personal

BUYER PREPARATION

finances. They have no outstanding credit card debt and drive a five year old automobile that is paid off. The same $5,000.00 in monthly income with the same 40% equals the same $2,000.00 per month in maximum qualifying monthly debts.

$5,000.00 Monthly Gross Income	$2,000.00 Max Qualifying Debts
	- 0.00 Auto Payment.
X .40	- 0.00 Credit Card Debts
$2,000.00 Max. Monthly Obligations	$2,000.00 Qualifying House Payment

This family is ready to purchase a nice home and start building equity in their investment program. They will also receive favorable tax treatment on their Federal and State incomes taxes.

Let's assume that they bought a house for $250,000.00 and it appreciates at 10% per year. That is $25,000 for the first year, $27,250 for the second year, $30,250 for the third, $33,275 for the fourth and $36,602 for the fifth for a total of $152,625.00 in property appreciation in 5 years. The property value has increased from $250,000 to $402,625. The second family now has equity in a home which should continue to appreciate. The first family may be making their last payments on their automobiles and hopefully they have been collecting rent receipts from me. They will not have ownership of a home or equity, but they will have two older vehicles and a handful of rent receipts. However, they will have been living the "good life" for the last five years.

There is no way of actually knowing what monthly consumer debt actually costs the consumer over their lifetimes. It is a lot more than just the actual combined monthly payments of the debts, even though that amount is incredible. Consumer debt tends to be debt incurred in purchasing items for consumption and items that depreciate in value. Mortgage debt is used for purchasing real estate which should appreciate in value.

Debt is a trap which man sets and baits himself, and then deliberately gets into.

- JOSH BILLINGS

Now, let's compare consumer debt to investment debt and see what kind of difference we get. Assume that we have $1,000,000.00 in investment mortgages on our credit report.

It does not matter how many properties we own, their combined indebtedness totals $1,000,000.00. We are also going to assume that we have 10% equity in the properties, so their combined market value will be $1,111,111.00 ($1,000,000.00 divided by .90).

We are going to assume that the properties do not have any negative or positive cash flow. That means that the rent the tenants are paying is just enough to cover the house payments. We have the tenants making the payments on the $1,000,000.00 debt, and we get to lower our income taxes by the amount of any depreciation and additional taxes write offs.

The rich aren't like us, they pay less taxes.

- PETER DE VRIES

The biggest advantage is that we, the borrower, get to watch our net worth increase as the value of the property increases. So, $1,111,111.00 times 10% equals $111,111.00, and that is just the increase in value the first year. It increases even more each year. The appreciation is based on the total value of the property not on just the mortgage amount. If each $1,000,000.00 of property will increase in value by $100,000.00 with 10% appreciation, how many millions would you like to own?

It took me years to get one million dollars in mortgage debt. You cannot just run out and borrow $1,000,000.00; you need to be able to prove to the investors that you can manage that level of debt. I had excellent credit and years of management experience, but it takes time and planning to be able to work up to that level of debt. At that time houses did not cost nearly as much as they do today.

Now when I buy two houses per year, I may spend $1,000,000.00 for the two properties. Due to the changing property values, it took years to accomplish what I can now do very easily in one year. It is like a snow ball rolling down the side of a hill. It gets bigger and bigger as it rolls. I tell everyone that I created the "Cash Snow Ball," and now I just continue feeding it and let it grow.

You can create your own "Cash Snow Ball," if you avoid burying yourself in consumer debt, plan smart and work your plan. I promise you can do it, it is not that difficult, just get a plan together and get started as soon as possible.

In a calendar year, 75% of the time the rates are higher the first six months of the year and 90% of the time the rates are lowest in November and December. Properly managing your mortgage debt is just important as managing your consumer debts. The big difference is that proper mortgage management can make you wealthy while consumer debt makes someone else wealthy.

QUICK REVIEW

1. All contractual monthly debt, including your house payment should not exceed 40% of your monthly income.
2. Consumer debt requires 2.5 times that amount in monthly income to offset monthly payments.
3. It is critical to keep your monthly debt as low as possible if you want to purchase real estate.
4. Consumer debt tends to be debt incurred in purchasing items that depreciate in value, while mortgage debt is for purchasing real estate that should appreciate in value.

Having a dream isn't stupid...
It's not having a dream that's stupid.

– ANON

INSIGHT 20

You Must Understand Your Mortgage Options.

During the Great Depression the banking system in the U.S. collapsed, resulting in massive foreclosures on homes and businesses. At the time, standardization in housing did not exist. Most homes did not have electricity or inside plumbing. In 1934, the Federal Banking System was restructured. The National Housing Act of 1934 was passed and the Federal Housing Administration (FHA) was created.

The FHA was designed to regulate lending practices—the rate of interest and terms of mortgages. The standardization in down payment requirements and the standardization in quality of construction made it far easier for millions of people to purchase homes. It also vastly increased the production and supply of modern housing in this country.

In 1965, the Federal Housing Administration became part of the Department of Housing and Urban Development (HUD). Since 1934, the two departments have insured over 34 million home mortgages and 47,000 multifamily projects. The Federal Housing Administration is completely funded by the borrowers that utilize its services at no cost to taxpayers.

The effect of the Federal Housing Authority has been to increase the size of the housing market and indeed housing has become a cornerstone of our economy. Now the greatest concentration of HUD housing is in the minority populations and in inner cities.

The Department of Veterans Affairs was established in 1930 to consolidate and coordinate government activities affecting war veterans. The VA experienced very rapid growth after the end of World War 2, when 16 million veterans returned home from the war. The G.I Bill, which included education and housing benefits, became available to veterans. The V.A. established its lending criteria and housing guidelines. This program also created a huge demand for new housing by the returning veterans. These two programs created the basis of our existing housing industry as we know it today is and often referred to as the government loan programs.

The real giants in the housing industry today are Federal National Mortgage Association referred to as Fannie Mae (FNMA) and The Federal Home Loan Mortgage Corporation referred to as Freddie Mac (FHMC). The Federal National Mortgage Association was created in 1938 as part of the Franklin Roosevelt's New Deal Programs.

Fannie Mae originally operated like a savings and loan, allowing home buyers to borrow money at low interest rates. This eventually led to the creation of what is now known as the secondary market. Fannie Mae is able to borrow money on the secondary market at low rates because the loans are backed by the U.S. Government. Borrowing money at lower rates and then lending it to home buyers at higher rates has allowed Fannie Mae to operate at a profit.

Fannie Mae had a monopoly situation until 1968, when Lyndon Johnson privatized it to remove it from the national budget. It began operating as a Government Sponsored Enterprise (GSE) generating profits for stockholders and protected financially by the Federal government. The second GSE, Freddie Mac, was created by Congress in 1970. These two organizations control about 90% of the nation's secondary mortgage market. Their combined debt totals about 46% of the current national debt.

Commercial banks also generate mortgages which are not sold on the normal secondary market. These loans are called Portfolio Loans. Banks fund the loans with the intention of keeping them for at least the first year, or selling them directly to Wall Street as mortgage backed securities in the mortgage industry. These loans are referred to as conventional loans as opposed to government loans.

This gives you a quick history and background of the mortgage industry. The loan products that we are going to be primarily concerned with are the conventional loans. The government programs are still available, however their loan limitations and high costs have severely limited their use on the east and west coasts. The house prices on the coasts are currently two to three times the maximum FHA loan limits.

The standard term for a mortgage is 10, 15, 20, 25, 30, 40 and 50 years. The most common term by far is a loan amortized over 30 years. The most quoted loan is a 30 year fixed. That is the interest rate stays the same for the entire 30 year amortized life of the loan. If you refer back to the normal yield curve, you will remember that the farther out you go on the yield curve the higher the expected bond yield. The same applies to a mortgage: longer terms are usually at higher rates.

The higher the interest rate, the more expensive a loan becomes over its life to the borrower. Normally, the most expensive loan is a 40 year fixed mortgage. Loans with shorter terms or adjustable rates are normally written for a lower rate of interest. That is not always the case. At times, all of the loans, fixed or adjustable, might bear the same interest rate.

Why are the rates all the same at times? The yield curve is either flat or slightly reversed. The farther out you go on the yield curve, the bond rates are declining. The more bond rates decline as you go out on the yield curve, the stronger the indication that we may be headed into a recession. Remember, a recession is an excellent time to invest.

In a normal year, I would offer a client a choice between a thirty year fixed at a certain interest rate and an adjustable loan of various terms and conditions. I would inform the customer that the 30 year fixed bore the higher interest rate because the investor was committing the money for the next 30 years. When the rates are all the same, most of my clients would opt for the 30 year fixed even though they know they will not have the loan for the next 30 years.

The 30 year fixed loan is the most popular and comes in two different types. The first is the fully amortized loan with equal payments for the entire life of the loan. The second 30 year fixed is "interest only" payments for the first 10 years, and the balance is amortized over the remaining 20 year life of the loan. This gives the borrower lower payments for the first 10 years because they are only required to pay the interest on the loan, not any of the principle.

I prefer the interest only loan for two reasons. The first, of course, is the lower payments for the first 10 years. There is virtually no chance that I will have that loan for more than 4 or 5 years, let alone 10 years. The second reason is that I have locked in a fixed interest rate that is not going to change over the life of the loan. This is a great loan product for someone who cannot sleep at night for worrying about an adjustable rate loan on his house but wants a lower payment for the first few years. With this type of loan, you have the flexibility to make a fully amortized payment anytime during the interest only portion of the loan or make a payment on the principal at any time without paying a penalty.

The second major type of loan is an adjustable interest rate loan. The loan is written for a specified time period but the interest rate will change during the term of the loan. The interest rate may be fixed for as short a time period as one month, six months, one year, 3 years, 5 years, 7 years or 10 years.

The advantage of the second type of loan is normally the shorter the time period that the interest rate is fixed the lower the interest rate will be while it is fixed. The rates will adjust based on an adjustable index plus a fixed margin. These indices basically show the costs of borrowing money based on a particular financial criterion. A typical index may be U.S Treasury, Libor, COFI, MTA or many other indices. Then a fixed margin is added to that index to determine the borrower's final interest rate (adjustable index plus fixed margin equals the interest rate).

A loan that has a fixed time period and then adjusts is often referred to as a hybrid loan. Many adjustable loans will contain a conversion clause which allows it to be converted to a fixed interest rate normally on the first five anniversary dates of the loan.

Most borrowers know that they will not have the same mortgage for 30 years. The average life of a loan is about 4 to 6 years before it is paid off either because the owner sells the property or it is refinanced with another mortgage. We have had twenty-five years of declining interest rates, and it is very hard to find a reason not to refinance a mortgage several times over that time period.

The third type of mortgage is an adjustable loan that has an adjustable interest rate as well as a choice of payments, called "an option pay loan". They normally have four payment choices each month. The first is called "a minimum payment," usually about 1 % to 4% of the loan amount. This percentage number has nothing to do with the interest rate. The interest rate will be an adjustable rate that may change each month. The minimum payment does not cover all of the interest. If the borrower only makes the minimum payment the loan will be a negative amortized loan and the balance of the loan will go up each month. Typically, these loans will cap out at 115% of the original loan amount after 3 to 5 years if the borrower only makes the minimum monthly payment. Once the balance reaches the 115% mark, the loan will be recast based on the new balance and amortized over the remaining life of the loan. Each 5 year period the loan will be re-evaluated and recast over the remaining life of the loan.

Each month the borrower gets a choice of making the minimum payment, interest only, 15 year amortization or a 30 year amortization. If the borrower makes any of the payments other than the minimum payment, the loan will not have negative amortization. This loan is very popular in states with very expensive real estate such as California. I have been told that about 60% of all new mortgages in California are option pay loans.

The adjustable and option pay loans have been getting a lot of negative press lately. They have been referred to as "new exotic mortgages" that are getting ready to implode because of the slowdown in the real estate industry. The first thing to note is that these "new mortgages" have been around for decades and have never been blamed on any real estate market collapse. In fact, prior to FHA and VA establishing national guidelines for amortizing mortgages, loans were usually only written for 1, 2 or maybe 5 years before they had to be paid off in full, and most of them were "interest only" loans. These products are not new in the housing industry.

The borrower always has several options available to them if he gets into a financial bind no matter what kind of loan that he may have on the property. From my experience, the loan product on the house seldom has anything to do with the borrowers getting into a financial bind. That is normally caused by other financial factors in their lives.

Sub-prime loans are the one exception; they have a short time period, usually 2 or 3 years, in which the interest rate is fixed at a teaser rate that is below the market rate at the time of closing. After the fixed time period the interest rate will increase by 4 to 6 % and the loans typically will have 6 months interest as a pre-payment penalty. That means if the loan is refinanced or paid off early (for any reason) the lender will charge 6 months interest as a pay off penalty. This loan can work fine as long as the property continues to appreciate in value. If it does not, it will become a financial trap that the borrower cannot escape.

Sub-prime loans are a disaster in real estate markets around the country. They are costing tens of thousands of home owners their homes, and now the monster has turned on the financial institutions that created and promoted the creature. The big difference is that the government will let the individual home owners fail; they will be wiped out financially and many will be forced to file bankruptcy. However, the financial institutions that created the monster will be saved and protected by the government; they will not be allowed to go bankrupt. Yes, many of them will be taken over by other institutions, but they will not be forced into bankruptcy and suffer the same fate as the homeowners.

As an investor you need to understand that market contractions for any reason create new and exciting opportunities for the investors that are able and willing to take advantage of them. A market contraction is really a redistribution of wealth within a market group. A lot of individuals will lose a lot of money or become insolvent while others will recognize the opportunities and become wealthy from the market contraction. Don't let the newspaper headlines intimidate you into inaction. Realize that new opportunities are going to be created for those that recognize and move fast on them. If the owners are in a financial bind, they may be able to sell the property or refinance it into a different loan product. They may want to consider a "cash-out loan", where they pull cash out of their equity. I do not recommend this unless it solves a financial problem that they may have encountered or if they want to invest in other property. I use my home equity line of credit (HELOC) when I need to raise some cash quickly. It doesn't cost anything to have the HELOC available for future use.

The "option pay loans" are complicated loans and hard for borrowers to understand. Personally, I do not believe that most loan officers understand the loan product as well as they should. Also, the advertising over radio and TV regarding all loan products is completely misleading (legal, but misleading). It is important for the consumers to make sure that they understand the terms and conditions of the loan. The old adage of "if it sounds too good to be true it probably is," still applies.

The terms and conditions are clearly spelled out on the note. If the borrowers have concerns, they should ask to see a blank copy of the note before agreeing to accept the loan product. They can study the blank note in detail before they agree to the loan. If the loan originator will not provide a blank copy to study, it is time to find another loan officer. After reading the blank copy, ask any questions that you may have about the loan product. Take it to your C.P.A. or your attorney if you still have concerns. These are legal documents that you will be signing: understand what you are signing because those documents have serious legal and financial ramifications.

None of the loan products (except most sub-prime) are bad products; they are simply different products that serve different needs. I have used all of the loan products myself, and I think that all of them have a place in the loan business. If there was not a need for the product, it would simply cease to exist in the marketplace.

There are borrowers who do not want to take the time to examine the loan product, and there are loan originators who do not take the proper time to explain the product and make sure that the borrowers understand it. I am convinced many borrowers only hear what they want to hear and ignore what they do not want to hear. They operate on the assumption that if they do not know of a potential problem, then there must not be one. As a borrower, you need to understand that a loan officer is not your agent in a transaction, and they do not legally represent the borrower. They are employed by the lender. Your REALTOR® or attorney is usually your agent in a real estate purchase transaction.

Many loan officers operate on the theory that they will conduct business with the customer only one time, then they are on to the next customer. Their concern is how much they are going to earn from each transaction, not how satisfied the customer will be. I have been in the business full-time for 17 years, and I know how many loan officers operate. Between the borrower's complete denial and the loan originators short-sightedness, it is no wonder that problems occur in the industry. The Federal Government requires that any applicant for a mortgage must receive a "Good Faith Estimate" and a "Truth in Lending" within three business days of submitting an application for a loan. The Good Faith Estimate is just what it says; it is a good estimate of what the borrowers closing costs should be and a breakdown of the monthly payment. In our office, we are very seldom off more than $100.00 on a good faith estimate, and this includes the closing costs and the borrower's prepays for their new impound account.

The Truth in Lending calculates the true costs of the loan including the interest rate and the closing costs in obtaining the loan. This calculation is called the "Annual Percentage Rate" or "APR." This information allows you to compare the costs of one loan against another loan. There is no way that the average consumer could correctly compare one loan against another without comparing the APR's of the two products.

The purpose of the Truth in Lending form is to prevent lenders from hiding fees and upfront costs while advertising misleading low interest rates. The problem with APR calculations is that the method of calculating has never been clearly defined. Lenders use different fees and charges in calculating their APR. The APR is also based on the assumption that the borrower is going to keep the loan for the full period of the loan, which seldom happens in the real world.

The APR does not require disclosure of balloon payments or pre-payment penalties, and ARM loans are calculated on the assumption that the index never changes, which is always going to be a false assumption. APR calculations are definitely not perfect, but they are better than nothing. If the borrowers understand the weak points, APRs can be of tremendous value in comparing loans.

As a borrower, you should understand the Good Faith Estimate and Truth in Lending are not loan approvals, and the lender is not locked into the estimates. The final figures and product may be entirely different than the original documents reflected. Until you have a "Loan Approval" and a "Lock" on the interest rate, it can change at any time.

A lender's letter of approval helps create credibility when it accompanies an offer to purchase real estate. In our area, most REALTORS® want the buyers approved by a lender before they even write an offer to purchase. They do not want to be wasting everyone's time on an offer from a buyer that may or may not be able to qualify for a mortgage. Sometimes there may be derogatory items on the borrower's credit report that must be resolved before loan approval takes place. The approval may take several weeks or months to resolve, and the sellers are not going to want to have their property off the market during the interim while waiting for the borrowers to get loan approval. It is best to take it step at a time and get loan approval before trying to purchase.

I get calls just about every day from potential borrowers who have heard or seen some kind of advertising on radio, TV or in a newspaper about some great interest rate on a fabulous loan product. I ask the client what is the APR and what are the total closing costs involved in the ad. They have absolutely no idea because that information is not provided in the ad. The only way that you can compare the two programs is with a Good Faith Estimate and a Truth in Lending and that is why they are required by State and Federal Laws. That is why I tell everyone the ads are legal, but they are totally misleading in their content. There is not one single product in the market that is not available to nearly all loan originators. The loan products are not made available to just one company as the ads would like us to assume; they are marketed all over the country.

BUYER PREPARATION

The Federal Reserve board developed a new consumer handbook on adjustable rate mortgages which does an excellent job of explaining them. It has been updated to include a section on option pay loans. This is a very thorough handbook that I highly recommend. You can access the information online and view or print this excellent consumer handbook. The website is **www.federalreserve.gov/pubs/arms/arms_english.htm**.

QUICK REVIEW

1. There are many types of mortgage options to fit different buyers' needs.
2. The higher the interest rate, the more expensive a loan becomes.
3. Due to the yield curve, a longer-term loan normally has a higher interest rate.
4. Use the Truth in Lending and the Good Faith Estimate to help you compare the loan products.
5. Make sure you understand the products you are choosing.
6. Get loan approval before making an offer on a property.

INSIGHT 21

There is No Such Thing as a "No Costs Mortgage."

It is hard to open a newspaper or watch TV without getting blasted with ads about some lender's "No Costs Mortgage" products. Let's look at the true story behind these ads. Most costs associated with a new mortgage are what we call third party costs. That means the money does not go to the lender. The money is collected at closing to pay for items like credit reports, appraisals, and escrow and title fees. These charges are exactly the same for every lender and for each loan. The appraiser gets paid, title gets paid, escrow gets paid and credit reporting agencies get paid. The lender cannot charge more for the service than what it actually costs.

The difference is in who technically pays for them, the borrower or the lender.

Everyone knows that the borrower is the party that actually winds up paying for the costs of the loan. It is just like a new car dealer giving the buyer a cash rebate at the time of purchase. Whose cash is he giving to the borrower? The borrower is getting the cash back that the dealer overcharged for the vehicle.

When a lender advertises a "No Costs Loan," they are not closing the loan and paying the costs out of their own pockets. Those costs have to be paid. If the lender paid the costs, they would be out of business in a very short time period. How do they cover the costs of the loan? It is very simple. They raise the interest rate above the going market rate. All lenders in the United States operate this way. They simply raise the borrower's interest rate to cover the cost of the originating the loan. The costs of a loan in Arizona are about 2.0% of the loan amount. That means a $200,000 loan is going to cost about $4,000.00 and that amount is not going to vary unless the lender is charging additional discount points (discount points will be covered later).

To cover the $4,000.00 in costs, the lender will have to raise the interest rate about 5/8% above the market rate at the time of the loan closing. That will raise the monthly payment on a $200,000.00 loan amortized over 30 years by $81.52 per month.

If you take the $4,000 and divide it by the $81.52, it will take 49 months to reach the break-even point. If the borrower is going to pay the loan off in less than 49 months, and there is not a pre-payment penalty, the lender paid closing costs loan is a good deal for the borrower. If the borrower is going to keep the loan for longer than 49 months, it is not a good deal for the borrower. If you multiply the $81.52 by 360 months (30 years), you will find that your total payments for the life of the loan are $29,347.20 higher than if the borrower had paid his own closing costs of $4,000 up front.

The consumer needs to understand the difference and how that difference affects his loan. I have no problem providing a lender paid closing costs loan to a borrower, but I will work the loan up both ways and show the borrower the differences. That means I will prepare a Good Faith Estimate and a Truth in Lending for both loan products because I want the consumer to see the actual differences in the two loans. That is exactly what an informed consumer should expect from a loan originator. Ask to be shown the differences in black and white. A "lender paid closing costs loan" will costs tens of thousands of dollars more over the life of the loan versus the borrower paying their own normal closing costs up front.

A pre-payment penalty is a charge that the lender charges the borrower when they decide to pay off a loan before a specified time period. The penalty is usually in effect for one to three years after the loan is originated. It is simply pre-paid interest that the lender charges because the loan is being paid off early. I do not recommend pre-payment penalty on most loans. However, some types of loans always have pre-payment penalties. The sub-prime loans normally have a 2 to 3 year pre-payment penalty, and the option pay loans usually have a pre-payment that varies between 1 and 3 years.

The biggest concern that I have with pre-payment penalties is that if interest rates decline, the consumer may not be able to capitalize on the lower rates because of a pre-pay penalty. Also, most of the loans have a low teaser rate for the first couple of years. Then the rate will increase dramatically, and the borrower may not qualify to refinance at a lower rate. If the borrower needs to sell early for any reason, he will have to pay the pre-payment penalty at closing, which may be several thousand dollars.

Discount points are typically a waste of the borrower's money and should be considered only in very unusual situations. Discount points are a fee charged by some lenders as normal lender charges. A discount point is 1% of the loan amount, and it is considered pre-paid interest. A discount point should lower the interest rate below the going market rate for that loan product at the time of the loan closing. The only time that I have ever charged a discount point was when the borrower insisted upon buying the rate down to a lower level. In my opinion, discount points are a waste of the borrower's money and should be avoided whenever possible.

Points paid at the purchase of an owner-occupied home can be deducted as pre-paid interest from tax returns in the year that they were paid. Points paid for a refinance must be amortized over the life of the loan. When you pay points for a loan, if you should refinance or sell in the future, you are going to lose the value of the points. It typically takes about 5 or 6 years to reach the break even point on a loan to cover the cost of the discount points. Most loans are paid off after 2 to 4 years because the borrower either refinances or sells the property.

A *Pre-qualification* consists of a loan officer taking verbal information from a potential borrower and determining whether he can qualify for a loan. What is the value of this document? It's worthless.

A *Loan Status Report* consists of a loan officer actually taking the borrower's application and running his tri-merged credit report. What is the value of this document? Fair to Medium.

A *Pre-approval* by a lender consists of taking his application, running the tri-merged credit report and verifying the information. The value is good for the buyer, but property still needs to be approved.

An *Approval* by a lender consists of all of the above submitted to underwriting and approved. The property still needs to be approved, and the final approval is contingent upon an acceptable property appraisal.

Final Approval consists of borrower approved, property approved and all loan conditions cleared.

QUICK REVIEW

1. There is no such thing as a "No Costs Mortgage." The costs are hidden in the higher interest rate that the borrower pays.
2. Pre-payment penalties and discount points are best avoided.
3. Whatever products the buyer is considering should be clearly explained and compared. Loan products are continually changing.

INSIGHT 22

Use a Professional Full Time REALTOR® and Loan Officer.

Let's assume that you are ready to start your investment program and buy your first home. The first thing to do is find an experienced REALTOR® and loan officer. If you know someone who has recently purchased a home, maybe they can possibly refer you to a qualified person. You can look in the newspaper, on-line, phone books, trade publications, and so forth. Let's assume that you have someone in mind, and you have an appointment set up with them.

Ideally, the first person that you would want to meet is a professional full time loan officer. First you need to know if the loan officer is someone with whom you can build a comfortable working relationship. Secondly, the loan officer should be able to tell you exactly the type and amount of a loan for which you can qualify.

Let the loan officer introduce himself, and tell you about his loan experience and about his company. Does he work for a bank, mortgage broker, or a mortgage bank? There are significant differences between the various companies. *How much experience does the loan officer have, what are his professional credentials, and how much experience does he have working with investors? Most importantly, is he an investor himself? Does he personally own investment property? If not, why not? You need to work with professionals that "talk the talk and walk the walk."*

Please, do not start working with a part-time person who has virtually no experience in the business. Buying real estate is probably the largest business transaction you will ever make in you entire life, and you need to do it right. You need experienced professionals to help you make the best possible business decisions. Mistakes cost you time and money, two things that you do not want to waste. If you cannot see the truth in this statement, perhaps you should reconsider whether or not you are really ready to make a sound business decision in regards to purchasing a property.

Let's start with a normal retail bank where you have your checking and savings accounts. I use my bank for my business accounts and for home equity lines of credit (HELOC) on each of my properties. I do not use my bank for mortgages on my properties because they are not very good at originating mortgages, they will not have many loan programs, and normally their loans are more expensive than the loans provided by mortgage brokers or mortgage banks.

A bank will typically have about eight or nine different loan products for mortgages and normally only qualify the borrowers "full doc," that is, full documentation of income for the last two years. If you are a full time W2 employee this may not be a concern for you, but if you are self-employed, commissioned, or retired, it could be a major problem. Banks are not very flexible. You either meet their guidelines for a loan or you will be declined.

I have found that they also charge a higher rate of interest than the rest of the industry. They can do so because they know a large percentage of their customers will only go to their bank for a loan, and the bank takes advantage of that fact. I am in the mortgage business and whenever a customer tells me that they are going to compare my rates against his bank's rates, I always encourage them to do so. I let his bank sell my services to the customer. I will always have lower rates than a bank, more experience, and a larger selection of loan programs.

The other major problem with a bank's loan officer is that he or she probably will not have much experience. Two months before you requested information about a loan, he/she may have been processing credit card applications or car loans, Plus, he/she probably does not have any authority in deciding if the loan is going to get approved or not. He or she takes the application from the borrower and sends it off to underwriting, wherever that may be. Underwriting makes a decision and lets the loan officer know what the findings are, end of story.

A mortgage broker should have lower interest rates and fees and a much wider selection of loan products. Mortgages are rated from "A Paper" to "D Paper", depending upon the borrower's credit history. A broker should be able to accommodate a borrower from A paper to D paper. The lower the credit grade, the higher the interest rate will be since the risk factors to the lender are higher. A good broker may suggest things to increase your credit scores. As previously mentioned, sometimes you can increase the scores by 50, 70 or even 100 points. A better credit score could save the borrower thousands of dollars in interest over the life of the loan. I have done this hundreds of times for my customers. I have never heard of a bank employee ever helping a borrower increase their credit scores.

A *mortgage broker* never funds a loan in his company's name. In other words they do not fund the loan themselves. They originate the loan and must meet the final lender's underwriting guidelines. The final lender will provide the funds to close the loan. A broker never uses his or her own funds to complete the transaction.

A *mortgage banker* normally originates, underwrites, and funds the loan with the bank's money. A mortgage banker normally does not use a third party to fund the transaction. However, a mortgage banker may also act as a mortgage broker, if he chooses to do so. The advantage of using a mortgage banker is that the transaction can usually move faster and smoother because the bank is using its own underwriting guidelines and its own monies. If the mortgage bank does not have the type of loan that my client needs, I can probably broker it out to an investor who does specialize in that type of loan product. This gives the client the largest possible choice of loan products to choose from, which can be very important in a transaction.

Now that you understand some of the differences between the companies, let's determine if the loan officer is right for you and your goals. If you are buying a home in which to live, this is normally a very straightforward transaction. It is a matter of determining which loan program best fits your needs, such as the amount of down payment and the monthly payment. You may decide to take a thirty year fixed or an adjustable loan product. It is best if you are receptive to listening to various loan programs without pre-judging them. Do not let the local newspaper articles lead you in a wrong direction. No one can determine which loan product is best for you until they have looked at your entire financial situation and have an understanding of the current mortgage market.

BUYER PREPARATION

If you are an investor (or thinking of becoming one) you need to be very selective in choosing a loan officer. Investor loans may be underwritten differently than other loans, and the loan products may be more sophisticated than the normal home owner would require. Many investors are self-employed or commissioned salespeople, and they usually have more complicated applications. They may also want specialized loan products that reduce their monthly payments for the first couple of years because of concern about negative cash flow.

The biggest reason I recommend experienced full-time loan officers that own investment properties is because they have "been there, done that". Their experience can be extremely valuable to you in helping you choose loan products, and properties to purchase, as well as having management ideas. They can share with you what has worked for them and what has not. Take advantage of their experience; it should not cost you one cent more than using someone who has absolutely no experience with investment properties. It could save you thousands of dollars in mistakes. Remember that real estate is a huge investment. You want as much experienced help as you can find. I still count on my customers to advise me, just as I advise them. Imagine all of the years of experience that my investors share with me and that I share with them. Together we share decades of experience, and that is absolutely priceless information for all of us. It is also information that applies right here in our local markets. If you do not use any other advice in this book, this advice alone could easily be worth several thousand times what you paid for it.

The next most important advice in this book (if you are an investor) is to work with a full-time professional REALTOR® who has experience working with investors and who owns investment properties himself. Again, their experience is invaluable to you as an investor. I use REALTORS® to represent me when I buy properties. There are brokers and then there are BROKERS, and they are not the same. They may have the same license and they may both have twenty years of experience, but do they have experience as real estate investors?

Realtors spend a lot of time in training classes; however, most of that training pertains to preventing their broker from getting sued or thrown in jail instead of learning about real estate investment concepts.

According to the National Association of REALTORS®, only about 4% of all licensed REALTORS® own property other than that in which they live. REALTORS® are commissioned salespeople, and they are always looking for that next commission check. They do not have a reputation for being long term investors. I have known hundreds of REALTORS® over the last three and a half decades, and only a handful ever invested in property other than their owner-occupied homes. If you ask them why they haven't bought investment property most of them will say "they just don't have enough time for it". If they do not have time enough for their own investments, how much time are they going to spend assisting you with your investments when you need it? You want to work with experienced loan officers and REALTORS® that "talk the talk and walk the walk."

I would say most of the REALTORS® who have bought investment property were buying it for a "fast flip." They had no intention of holding on to it any longer than it would take to sell. This technique can make money, in a short time period and in a "hot market." But when that market quickly changes from "hot" to "stone cold dead," they can find themselves in serious financial straits. In a slow market, homes do not move fast, thus a REALTOR'S® income normally can take a serious dive. If they are making additional house payments on vacant investment properties, things can get very tight for them.

I am not writing this to be critical of REALTORS.® They are salespeople and that is how they make their living. The vast majority of them sincerely try to do the best job they can for their clients. If you are buying an owner-occupied home virtually any full time REALTORS® will do a great job for you. If you are buying investment property, it requires an entirely different approach to time and select the type of property you may wish to purchase. Remember that you are going to be living with the property for years. The REALTOR® will get paid and be done with the transaction at the close of escrow.

Knowledge plus experience create results.

When contemplating purchasing investment properties, you need a complete game plan. You need to know what type of property you want to buy, where you want to buy, and you need to be knowledgeable regarding the rental markets and the best types of non-owner financing. This requires more than just filling out a purchase contract. This requires real-life experience in the business.

If it is so easy that any REALTOR® can properly advise you on investment property, why do so few of them own investment properties? Why aren't they doing what they are trying to advise you to do? I can not imagine using a stock broker who does not own stocks. The same logic applies to your REALTOR® and loan officer. Use someone in the investment market who knows about the latest financing available for investors and has real-world experience with investment properties.

BUYER PREPARATION

Try to develop a team of experts you can work with and count on to give you accurate and up-to-date information. Their expertise is invaluable for you and your program, so get started in the right direction right out of the gate. This one idea can save you a fortune in lost opportunities that you may not discover on your own. Take the time to find the right people. It will save you a lot of time and money, and prevent a lot of grief down the road.

QUICK REVIEW

1. Work with professionals who have personal experience investing in real estate. You want professionals that "talk the talk and walk the walk".
2. Mortgage brokers and mortgage bankers usually offer more products less expensively than regular commercial banks.
3. Be open-minded about loan programs and learn from you loan officer.
4. Be knowledgeable regarding current real estate values.

The work will teach you how to do it.

— ESTONIAN PROVERB

INSIGHT 23

Your First Real Estate Purchase should be Owner-Occupied.

The easiest property to purchase is an owner-occupied home. Lenders are much more inclined to make a loan to a borrower who is going to live in the house. It is easier for the owner to maintain a home, since they will be occupying the property.

You will receive the greatest income tax deductions on an owner-occupied property. The owner is much more inclined to make improvements to the property, and it is a much safer investment for the lender because the owner will do everything possible to make sure that the property never gets foreclosed on by the lender.

Investment properties are six times more likely to be foreclosed on as owner-occupied homes. Owner-occupied purchases will receive a lower rate of interest on the mortgage and usually better loan terms, such as lower down payments. If your first purchase is an owner-occupied home, after 12 months you can legally convert that property to investment property. You will not need to refinance it. You can simply leave the existing first mortgage on the property.

The important thing is to get started with home ownership as soon as possible. The longer you own real estate, the greater the amount of appreciation that you will realize, and the more money you will save on income taxes. Two out of three Americans are home owners and that is the largest investment that most of them will make in their lives. Real estate accounts for over 95% of most family's total wealth at the time of their retirement.

Another great advantage with home ownership is that currently you can avoid capital gains taxes on a gain up to $250,000 for an individual or $500,000 for a couple if they have owner-occupied the property for at least two of the last five years.

To become a first-time investor, you may need to refinance your first property before converting it to an investment property. You could use the proceeds from a HELOC to purchase the second owner occupied home. Another approach would be to refinance the first home with a new first mortgage and pull cash out of the property with a higher loan amount. This loan would also be an owner-occupied loan as long as the borrower was still occupying the property at the time of the refinance. If you simply purchased a different owner-occupied house every couple of years and kept the original houses you could build up a very sizable estate after a few years. I know because that is exactly what I did when I was starting out. It is a very conservative approach which will work just as well for you and your family.

You can use this technique with all types of property from immaculate homes, fixer-ups, foreclosures, new homes and vacant houses. I always tried to purchase properties in an area I call my "service area", that is they were close to where I was living. I do not like the idea of driving for 45 minutes one way to work on or to show a house to a prospective tenant. I want them as close as I can get to minimize my driving time.

When writing an offer on a property, always include the following contingencies in the offer. *First, the property must appraise for the sales price or higher, if it does not appraise the buyer will not be locked into paying more for the property than it is actually worth.* The second contingency should be a termite clearance on the property from a licensed termite company. The third contingency should be for the buyer to approve of a property inspection report from a licensed property inspector. The inspection report should be paid for by the buyer.

QUICK REVIEW

1. Home ownership should be the most important part of your investment plan.
2. Once you own a home, you can start purchasing other properties to increase your investment.
3. When purchasing real estate, demand an appraisal, termite clearance, and inspection report.

INSIGHT 24

Real Estate should be a Long Term Investment.

If you are a serious long term investor, a slow market can be a wonderful opportunity for you to buy property. You may not be able to sell inventory in a slow market, but you should not be trying to do so. A depressed market is the best time to be buying because you can shop around and find some wonderful opportunities out there. You need to take a long term approach on investing in real estate, the same as if you're investing in the stock market. Just as there are better months to be buying real estate, there are better months to be selling. There are better years to be buying and better years to be selling. Do not fight the market, flow with it.

I do not know many stockbrokers who advocate investing on a short term basis, except for day traders. Most of us do not have the time or desire to devote to a career as a day trader. It is the same with real estate. Most of us do not have the time or the desire to devote all of our time to real estate investing. I do not advocate real estate as a replacement for your regular employment. Later, after several years of investing and the built-up equity, you may want to devote more of your time to real estate and less to your other career.

Take a long term perspective; be very conservative in your investing and avoid making major mistakes. I would rather pass up a golden opportunity that entails a lot of risk, versus making a more conservative investment with minimal risk. Remember you must be able to survive the slow markets? Anyone can make money in a fast market, but can they survive the switch from fast to slow. Never assume that the market conditions are going to continue in the same direction. They are not. The market is going to change direction, so be ready for the change.

If you are a long-term investor you can take advantage of the market conditions and make them work in your favor. Keep an eye on the interest rates and know the rates are going to impact the real estate market either in a positive or a negative direction. Interest rates have a huge impact on real estate and automobile sales. They do not impact the sale of groceries, clothes, or health care. Credit card purchases do not slow down with increased interest rates. Credit cards carry a higher rate of interest than housing or autos and are not sensitive to rate hikes.

The automobile manufacturers try to off set higher rates with incentives on their auto sales such as 0% interest, longer payout periods, or cash incentives. They just increase the price of the cars to cover the incentives. I have noticed over the years that the family's car payments are taking a bigger bite out of the family's budget and that bite is becoming larger ever year. The payments have stretched out to 7 years, are now higher than what house payment used to be, and the car payments last longer than the automobile.

The real estate industry has also tried to accommodate buyers of homes by lengthening the term of mortgages from the standard 30 year mortgage to 40 and 50 year mortgages. They have developed ARM products, interest-only, and negative amortization loans all in an attempt to make housing more affordable. The price of housing and automobiles are going to continue increasing over the years because the costs of labor and material are going to continue to increase.

I believe that when the Fed raises interest rates in the future to control the rate of inflation by slowing the economy, it may have a more dramatic effect on depressing housing than it has in the past. If that proves to be the case, there will be wider swings in the number of houses sold in the future. The swings from the bottom of the cycle to the top of the cycle could create huge movements in the number of homes sold. Why do I think that may happen?

Housing is directly tied into interest rates and the prices have dramatically increased. When the Fed raises rates, a combination of the two situations will have a devastating effect on housing. This does not mean that the demand for housing has disappeared or gone away. The population will continue growing at the same speed and those additional new people will still need housing. Thus, when the Fed drops the rates there will be even more pent-up demand for housing and prices should increase dramatically.

If you look at some high-priced cities, such as Los Angeles, over 60% of all single-family houses in LA are rental properties. There are fewer property owners who own several properties and more families that rent generation after generation. The same situation also applies in New York City, where most families do not even consider owning their own home. It may get to the point where the average family on the east and west coast will never own their own homes. It is estimated that 50% of the population lives within fifty miles of the east and west coasts, and that creates tremendous pricing pressure on that supply of housing.

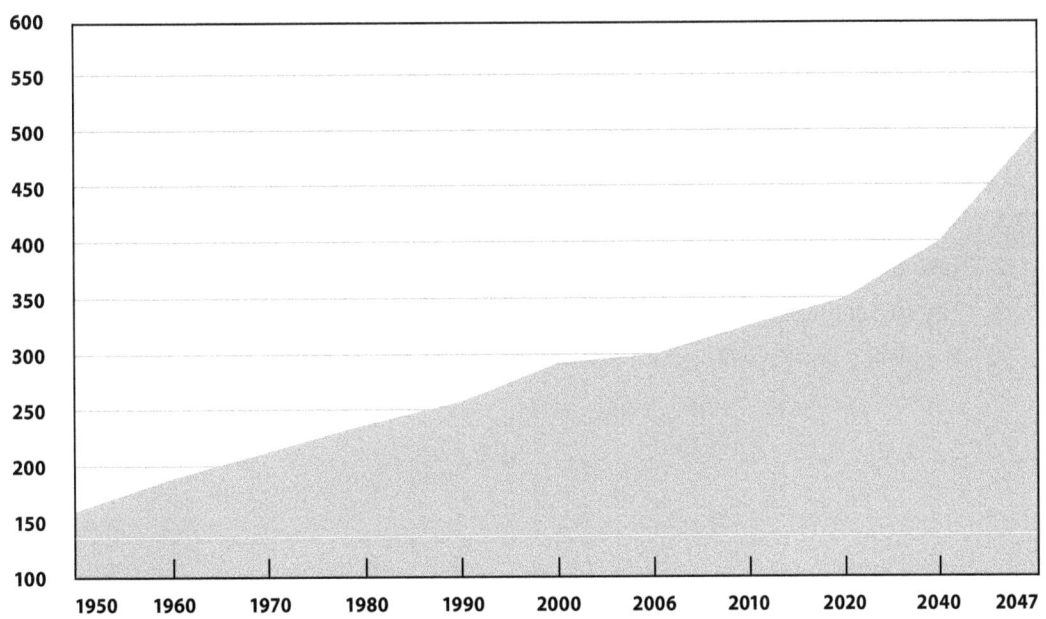

If the housing market starts making large swings in prices it should be a huge advantage for long-term investors who keep an eye on the markets and plan accordingly. Buy on the dips and be very reluctant to sell on the highs, but if you must sell, definitely sell into a strong market. If you own several properties it is not hard to pull equity out to handle any cash requirement that you may encounter. Rather than selling in a slow market, pull some cash out of your houses and wait until the market rebounds before selling.

Rates are high in an inflationary market and a shrewd investor that is knowledgeable of the market situation can make a lot of money because he knows that there will be motivated sellers who want to sell and/or must sell at just about any price.

Inflationary pressures can also work in the investor's favor because real estate normally increases in value 1 to 2% more than the rate of inflation.

Real estate should be a long-term investment and you need to be aware of what is happening in your marketplace to maximize your return. Do not panic because of market slow downs, keep your eye on the ball, look for some excellent buying opportunities, track interest rates, and enjoy what you are doing. Remember that you are either buying equity for yourself or you are renting and paying for equity for someone else.

QUICK REVIEW

1. Take a long-term approach to investing in real estate.
2. Take advantage of market conditions and make them work in your favor.
3. The east and west coasts are the most expensive places to purchase real estate.
4. Population growth will create a need for additional housing.

BUYER PREPARATION

INSIGHT 25

Hold On for the Long Term to Maximize Your Return.

Hold on for the long term if you want to maximize the return on your property. It costs a lot of money to buy (3% of sales price) and sell (10% of sales price) real estate. The buying and selling expenses can easily eat up two years of appreciation. If you bought the right kind of property in the right neighborhood, it should continue appreciating for a long time without incurring selling costs. Holding on for the long term combined with understanding the market movements should create a winning combination for you. You will know how and when to maximize your buying opportunities and also when to optimize your selling experience.

After you have built up some equity, you can refinance the property to access some of the equity. A refinance transaction also costs money (2.5% of loan amount), but you will still own an asset that is appreciating in value. Assume that you own a house that is worth $100,000.00. If that property appreciates at 10%, it will go up in value $10,000.00 in a year. Now assume that you owned several properties and their value totaled $1,000,000.00. With appreciation at 10%, they will go up $100,000.00 in value in one year.

It is not the number of properties that you own that is important. It is the total dollar value of those properties that count. All of the properties should be appreciating at some factor. It does not matter what the value is of any one property. What does matter is how you manage that property. A $100,000 house is not managed the same way a $1,000,000 house is managed. The tenants for the two properties are entirely different families, and the tenants for the expensive properties expect a different level of services with their rental.

I have rental properties occupied by tenants who have no intention of ever moving out of the house. I have never made a tenant move out before they were ready to move, assuming that they paid their rent on time and have taken care of the property. Also, I let the tenants make improvements to the properties if they choose, such as painting, landscaping, changing window coverings, etc.

It is their home and I want them to be happy while they are living there. Yes, I own the property, but they are the occupants. I simply have not considered moving a tenant out of a house so that I could sell it. If they are happy with the property, I want them to stay as long as they choose. I simply refinance the property and pull out some equity if I think that I am getting too much equity built up in the property. I do not want that much equity just sitting there and not working the way I desire.

I very seldom raise my rents once a tenant has moved in. The only exceptions are when the property taxes or insurance increase dramatically. If I get hit with an increase in taxes, which happens if you pick good properties, I write the tenants a letter, explain how much the taxes and insurance have increased, and I increase the rent by those amounts. I have never had a tenant complain about the increases or threaten to move out because they know that they are still paying less than market rents for the property. They also know that I have no control over how much property taxes or insurance increase.

If I have an excellent property in a great area and great tenants, why would I want to move them out and sell the property? If the property is making me money, why would I want to shoot myself in the foot—or the wallet? Just about every time that I have sold a house with existing tenants, I have regretted it, even though I had very good reasons for selling at the time.

A great tenant is an investor's best friend.

My original game plan was to eventually own ten rental properties plus my owner-occupied home. Then if I needed income, I could sell the first rental that I purchased and buy the eleventh property with part of the proceeds from the sale. That way, I would always have ten investment properties in my inventory. I planned to have more than enough equity in the first property to be able to buy another property and pull out whatever amount of additional cash that I needed at the time.

I think that this is still a good long-term plan. However, you don't need ten properties. You could do the same thing with two, five, ten, one hundred, or whatever number you want. Yes, I know investors that own anywhere from one to one hundred and fifty properties. I have now revised my game plan, and I do not believe that I will need to sell any properties.

Another reason to hold on for the long term is that it is difficult to time the market and know when it's the best time to sell. It is no fun placing a house on the market and then having the market come to a screeching halt. It is also not fun to sell a house, and then have the market blast off like a space rocket right after you sell. Both of these happen to homeowners, and it is not something that you want to have happen to you. Buy great properties in a great neighborhoods, manage them well, hang on for the long haul and you will be thrilled with the end results. You will have very saleable properties in any market, and you will minimize selling costs for your investment program.

If you buy great properties, for the right price, in a good location, you will not be able to afford to sell. The property should continue to appreciate so fast that you will not want to sell. If your house is appreciating at 10% and is worth $100,000, it will be worth $110,000 after one year, $121,000 after two years, and $133,100 after three years. The first year it appreciated $10,000 but the third year it appreciated $13,100. Will you really want to sell an asset that is making you that kind of money? Remember that you are also paying down the mortgage and lowering your taxable income.

That leads us to the "Rule of 72." If you take the number 72 and divide it by a number, such as 10 for 10%, the answer will give you the number of years it takes to double the value of that asset. Seventy two years divided by 10 equals 7.2 years, which equals the number of years it will take the asset to double in value. Seventy two years divided by 12 equals 6 years. At 12%, it will take 6 years for the asset to double in value. Now, what if you owned $5,000,000 worth of property, and it appreciated at 10% per annum? In 7.2 years the asset will double in value and be worth $10,000,000. Your net worth would have increased by $5,000,000.00 without selling or buying a property during that time period.

These are very realistic numbers in an economy that is growing in population and creating new jobs. Every day I read in the newspaper about various companies laying off thousands of their employees or terminating their employees' benefit plans. I can not imagine what people do after they have retired and have their retirement plan terminated by their past employer or union. I want to have control over my retirement income and not have it under the control of a third party.

You can create your own retirement plan and keep control of it yourself by using the ideas in this book. It is not very hard to create a plan that will take care of you and your family for the rest of your lives. It is just a matter of accepting responsibility for yourself and your financial future. You can do it and enjoy the satisfaction knowing you created your own financial future. The opportunities are there waiting for you to capitalize on them.

QUICK REVIEW

1. There are major costs when buying, selling, or refinancing a home, so holding on to a good property long-term is wise.
2. Keeping tenants involved and satisfied with the rental property they occupy is good business.
3. It is your responsibility to create your own financial future.

Wishing does not make a poor man rich.

— ARAB PROVERB

CHAPTER SIX

ADDITIONAL INTUITIVE CONCEPTS

INSIGHT 26

The Pro and Cons of Negative Cash Flow.

It is very difficult to buy property on the east and west coast with a minimum down payment and have the property rent for enough to cover the monthly mortgage payment, which includes principal, interest, taxes, and property insurance. The difference between the monthly payment and the rent can be either be a positive or a negative number. If the rent is more than the payment, the difference is referred to as positive cash flow. If the rent is less, it is referred to as negative cash flow.

Nearly everyone I talk to about investing in real estate wishes to avoid any negative cash flow, in addition, they want to make the minimum down payment when purchasing property. I can understand this desire, and I would be thrilled to be able to purchase property with a minimum down payment and start out with a positive cash flow. Unfortunately, that is not what the numbers will normally look like in a growing economy with appreciating real estate values.

You may be able to purchase property with a positive cash flow. However, consider the condition of the property and the neighborhood in which it is located. Do you really want to take on someone else's headaches and ongoing legal problems? Wouldn't you prefer to own property that is going to maximize your appreciation and total return on your investment?

Does this mean that you should not consider investing in real estate when you may have a negative cash flow situation? Let's take a closer look at what most people are accomplishing with their investment programs. On most of the applications that I see, the borrowers usually have a 401k, 403b or an IRA. The one thing that I consistently notice is that the return on these accounts is between 0% to a maximum of about 10% per annum. The ones that yield over 8% are rare. I see many accounts where the return is actually a negative figure.

I believe everyone should have a savings program and a source of liquid cash they can access when the need arises. I also think that everyone should be aware of what kind of return that they are actually receiving on these accounts. Some people keep $50,000 to $100,000 in their checking account and passbook savings account without realizing what kind of interest that these accounts are earning. The average checking account pays about ¼ of a percent interest on the average monthly balance for the account. Pass book saving accounts pay about 2% to 3% interest on the monthly balance. Many people have no idea that their money is earning such a small amount of interest.

Let's review this information: ¼% on your checking account balance, 2 to 3% on your savings account and probably 4 to 8% on your retirement account. This may be keeping up with the rate of inflation but not much more. What money did you use to make this kind of return? A payroll deduction is usually where it comes from, deductions right out of your paycheck. Yes, these amounts are subtracted from your taxable gross income for tax purposes, and some of you are fortunate enough to have an employer who will match a certain percentage of your payroll contribution. Does this mean that the money will never be subject to income taxes? Probably not, depending upon the type of account to which you are contributing. It will usually be taxed as the money is withdrawn from the account. The Internal Revenue Service always gets its share!

I see borrowers that are having $300, $500, $700 or even thousands deducted monthly from their paychecks. This money is "negative cash flow" because it is going into a savings account that is yielding terrible returns on the balances. I am not advocating that everyone should cancel their retirement accounts. However, I would like for you to consider some alternatives which should yield a much higher return on your investments.

Let's start with your checking and savings accounts. I have recommended these alternatives to many clients, and I have never had a complaint from anyone who has tried them. You can set up an on-line savings account with different banks that are tied directly with your current checking accounts. The money is deposited into your regular checking account, and then you transfer the funds from checking into an on-line savings account that is insured by FDIC, just like your regular bank account. When you think you may need part of the funds, simply transfer the monies from the on-line account back into your regular account. This transfer takes 2 or 3 days to complete. I have several of these accounts, and I normally receive about 5% interest on the balances. There is no minimum balance that you must maintain and you can go on-line anytime and check your balance and the interest rate. Five percent versus ¼ of a percent is a return that is 20 times greater than your checking account. It is also about twice as high as your

ADDITIONAL INTUITIVE CONCEPTS

passbook savings account. It also provides exactly the same protection as your regular bank. How can they pay this kind of return to you? They do not have the expense of maintaining branch offices all over the country. I have listed a couple of these banks in chapter 4.

Now, let's take a look at your payroll deductions for your investment accounts. Whatever amount that you are having deducted each month is added to your investment account balance plus any earned interest, dividends, and appreciation. Let's assume that you are receiving an 8% return on your investment (this is a lot higher than most accounts). To keep it simple, I am not going to add for any employer contribution. I don't see many employees receiving additional funds from their employers. I am also not going to consider how much you would lower your taxable income because real estate will provide a far larger income tax reduction than your combined payroll contributions will ever. I do not ever recommend investing in anything solely for the income tax deductions. However, real estate does provide significant tax deductions for a homeowner as well as investors. Consult with your CPA and have him demonstrate some of the tax benefits of real estate investing.

If you are deducting $500 per month from your paycheck, you will accumulate $500 times 12 or $6,000 per year. Let's assume 8% return per year, $6,000 times 8% equals $480 return per year. Divide that by 2, and your account balance will go up by approximately $240 for the first year. Remember, that your account did not have a $6,000 balance for the whole year. It takes a year to accumulate a $6,000 balance. At the end of the first year you will have approximately a $6,240 balance of which $6,000 was deducted from your pay checks ($6,000 of negative cash flow).

Now, let's assume that you could have purchased an investment property for the price of $300,000 and that you put 10% down and had a negative cash flow of $300 per month. If you picked out a good property in a nice area, you should easily get 8% appreciation per year. I personally have never received that low of an appreciation figure on any property which I purchased in a good area. Let's do the math. $300,000 times 8% equals $24,000 appreciation the first year, plus tax deductions, plus mortgage reduction. *Please note that the 8% appreciation was on the total value of the property, not just on the amount of cash invested.*

We made a $30,000 down payment at the time of purchase, and we incurred $300 per month of negative cash flow. The purchase price of $300,000 minus $30,000 down payment gave us a loan amount of $270,000. The $30,000 has not just disappeared; it is reflected as equity in the property.

However, there are costs incurred in having the $30,000 tied up in the property. After all, if it were in our investment account it would have earned 8% interest for the year. That costs is

$30,000 times 8% is $2,400 in lost opportunity earnings. Total costs should be $3,600 negative cash flow plus $2,400 in lost income for a total of $6,000. The first year return is $24,000 minus $6,000 equals a gain of $18,000 after expenses. We have a choice of $240 the first year from our 401k or $18,000 from our real estate investment. I have found that my negative cash flow usually diminishes over time as the market rents increase. I also purchase the properties below market value at the time of purchase. In a slow market, I can easily pick up $50,000, $75,000 to $100,000 in equity at the time of closing escrow. In the real world, these are extremely conservative numbers to demonstrate how much greater the return can be with a simple real estate investment plan. When I see applications with $100,000, $200,000, even $300,000 or more in accumulated funds that are earning practically nothing, it drives me nuts. When I see a large balance in a retirement account, I see a lot of "negative cash flow" that is earning practically nothing in comparison to what it could be earning.

I do not want anyone dumping their savings and retirement accounts, but with some minor changes, you can probably dramatically increase your return on your investment and retirement dollars. Perhaps you should be investing less into your retirement accounts and more into real estate. Think about the real difference between retirement deductions from your pay checks and negative cash flow on real estate investment. Which one gives by far the greatest return on your investment dollars, and which one gives the largest income tax deductions?

The purpose of an investment account is to build up equity or capital in the account. The capital will provide a source of income in the future when you may need it; the larger the estate, the larger or longer the flow of future income. I have a hard time seeing how the average family can save enough from payroll deductions to support themselves after retirement. I have had several customers who have built up their estates by $200,000 to $500,000 in just four or five years by investing in real estate. They made up their minds to move beyond what is simple and easy and handed to them by their employer without any effort on their part. If you truly want to improve your personal finances for yourself and your family, you must step up and get involved in real estate investing. The sooner you get started, the greater the potential rewards at the end;. The hardest part is simply making the commitment and getting started.

ADDITIONAL INTUITIVE CONCEPTS

QUICK REVIEW

1. Although positive cash flow is the goal for rental property, it is not always possible.
2. Take responsibility for making sure your money is maximizing its return to you.

INSIGHT 27

A Reverse Mortgage can be a Retiree's Financial Salvation.

If property appreciation and income tax deductions is not enough incentive for you to invest in real estate, how about adding in "lifetime income" as an incentive. I would like to discuss a different type of mortgage at this time. A reverse mortgage could become many people's most valuable financial asset in the future. A reverse mortgage can provide income to the property owner rather than the owner making house payments. They receive payments from their reverse mortgage. This product will become very important to many retirees in the future because it will provide them with additional income as long as they occupy the property. This additional income will not have any affect on their regular social security income and could very easily exceed the amounts of their social security checks.

A reverse mortgage is recorded against an owner occupied home, and it must be the first mortgage. Any other liens against the property must be paid off at the time of closing. Many seniors will own their house free and clear or owe a very small mortgage balance against their home. If they have over 60% equity (or more) in their property and the borrower is 62 or older, this may be a wonderful program for them. There are currently three sources of reverse mortgages: FHA, Fannie Mae and Financial Freedom. FHA has about 90% of all reverse mortgages at this time.

FHA is tied to the Treasury Bill Index plus a margin, and the loan limits are low and vary by county. The loans are based on the appraised value of the property, and the payments are determined by the age of the youngest of the borrowers and the loan amount. The age of the youngest of the borrowers will be used to determine the monthly payment because the lender is assuming that the youngest borrower will live in the house the longest. The loans are not cheap to set up, and FHA will allow the loan to be refinanced if the property appreciates in value. The lenders will also allow funds to be held in escrow at the time of closing to make home repairs such as air conditioning and heating repairs or replacing the roof. It is nice that a homeowner can go from having a house payment to no house payment and receive a monthly check each month.

The Fannie Mae program will loan a higher loan amount, currently up to $417,000. These loans are tied to the *one month secondary market certificate of deposit index*. They will allow a borrower to purchase a retirement home without a house payment, but they will need to put 50% down on the purchase.

Financial Freedom reverse mortgages have no maximum loan limits. They should be more attractive to owners of homes worth more than $500,000. These loans do not require the borrowers to have any income and their credit is only checked to verify that there are no liens against their property. The loans are based on the equity in the property and the age of the youngest borrower. You can check out the programs on the web at www.financialfreedom.com. These programs may become the cornerstone of many families' retirement programs. They can provide income to cover medical bills, drug expenses, and more.

QUICK REVIEW

1. A reverse mortgage can be an excellent source of income for someone 62 or older who has at least 50% equity in an owner-occupied home.
2. FHA, Fannie Mae, and Financial Freedom all offer reverse mortgages.

ADDITIONAL INTUITIVE CONCEPTS

INSIGHT 28

Always Remember That You are Buying to Sell.

Make certain that you are buying property that will be salable in the future, no matter what the market situation may be. There is always property selling, even in a horrible market. If you get caught in a situation where you must sell, you will be grateful that you bought properties that are very salable. If you are never going to sell, your children may want to sell, or your grandchildren. Someday, someone is going to want to sell that property. Selling begins with the purchasing. Make sure the property is located in a good neighborhood where people will want to live. Buy in a vibrant area which is creating new jobs, new freeways, good schools and excellent shopping facilities. Buy in an area where you would want to live and raise your family. If you would not live there, who do you expect to live there?

I am amazed at the number of people that want to become investors and want to start with the cheapest house on the market. They start out looking for a dump because it is going to be a rental property. What kind of tenant are you going to get to move into a destroyed dump?

The properties are usually located in the worst part of the community. Imagine owning a destroyed house in the worst part of town. The management problems will make your life miserable, and you will soon decide to sell the property, but to whom? You will soon discover why the house was the cheapest property on the market. Nobody wants the expense and headaches.

Do you really want to buy someone else's headaches?

Many investors start out with this type of property because of recommendations from their friends, relatives, or because they just want to buy the cheapest property. Stay with properties that are easy to manage, easy to rent, appreciate in value, and will be easy to sell. It makes life much more enjoyable. There are enough heartaches in life; you don't need to buy more of them.

When I am considering purchasing a property, I start out by analyzing it and breaking it down into two categories. The first category involves items of concern that I may have that cannot be changed or modified by the property owner, such as location, noise, traffic, electrical transmission wires, lack of parking or perhaps a very small backyard. These conditions cannot be changed or modified by the owner and will always affect the property's value. If I am not comfortable with these items and do not want to deal with them, I will not purchase the property.

The second category involves items of concern that can be changed or modified such as paint, landscaping, condition of roof, foundation repairs, termite damage, worn-out appliances and carpeting. These items can be fixed or repaired. The question then becomes one of cost. How much is it going to cost in both time and money to make the necessary repairs? If the numbers look good and the property would make an excellent investment, I will proceed with the purchase.

Remember that a property is affected by conditions around it, and you cannot move the house to another location. Just as a property can be affected by negative conditions, it can be affected by positive conditions. Maybe the city is going to build a new park in the area, pave some dirt streets or build a new school. These are conditions that could have a tremendous positive impact on the value of your property. It pays to keep abreast of what is happening in the immediate area and take note of any negative or positive situations that may be developing.

When contemplating selling a property, the house should be "staged" before placing it on the market. Staging can be very simple or it can be done by a professional stager, REALTOR® or an interior designer. I operate on the theory that most buyers start out looking for reasons to reject a property rather than looking for reasons to purchase. Eliminate the negatives before placing the property on the market.

Staging may include removing excess furniture, cleaning, and painting, replacing worn carpets, landscaping and eliminating clutter. You want to make the potential buyers very comfortable with the house and create an environment in which they will want to live. The purpose of the staging is to sell the house, sell it at the optimum price and sell it quickly.

Take the time to preview some new models homes in your area. Notice how there is very little furniture, nice décor and no dark spaces in the house. If you will take the time to count them, you may find 30 to 40 lights concealed in a room to eliminate any interior dark spaces. The rooms will always appear large, bright and spacious because of a limited amount of furniture and concealed lights. Try to use furniture that is the right size for the house, make the house look comfortable and stick to neutral colors that will not offend.

Do not ignore offending odors that may be present in a house such as those from pets or smoking. They can be an immediate turn-off for a lot of people. I have found when women are previewing houses, the first thing they seem to focus on are the kitchens and bathrooms. Make certain that the stove, cabinets, and bathrooms are clean.

The landscaping should be trimmed and have a neat appearance. Remove or trim any large plants or trees that are too close to the entry way of the house. The entryway should be clean and open with no obstructions blocking the path. Make sure that the front door is clean, painted and has as much eye appeal as possible. Curb appeal is extremely important in the selling of residential property. The decision to buy or not to buy is usually made before the potential purchasers enter the house.

QUICK REVIEW

1. Buy a quality property in a good location.
2. Be aware of what changes are happening in the area in which you want to purchase.
3. "Staging" a property will help you sell it for a high price and in a shorter time period.

INSIGHT 29

In a Slow Market, Property in the Outlying Areas Get Hit the Hardest.

In a major metropolitan area there will be houses built on the outside perimeter of the area. The further out the builders go, the cheaper they can buy the land to build their subdivisions. This means that the buyers can buy a house cheaper or buy a bigger house for the same price as a smaller house closer to town.

The problem with this strategy is that because they are out in an open area, it is easy for the builder, and all other builders, to buy additional land and subdivide it. There is nothing restricting how many houses can be built in the area. Consequently, the local markets in the outlying areas are saturated with new houses. You may find that it is extremely difficult to sell or rent because of the additional costs of driving the longer distance to a place of employment or services.

Once you purchase a new home, you will need to spend several thousand dollars for landscaping, window coverings, pools and other items. If you should need to sell and the builder is building and selling the same floor plan, or similar, your home is going to be overpriced in comparison to those of the builder. You will need to cover the costs of the house, plus improvements, plus the additional cost of selling. The builder will not have these additional costs, and he will offer large financial incentives to the prospective buyers that you will not be able to match.

Whenever I buy a new house in a subdivision, I assume that I will not be able to sell until the builder has completed the subdivision and has moved on to another location. I also assume that I will not get much appreciation until the builder has closed out the subdivision. If I get appreciation before the builder is done, great, but I am not going to count on it at the time of purchase.

As an investor, I have found that is very difficult to buy an investment property in an outlying area and rent the property out for the amount I need. Rents in the outlying areas are much lower than property rents closer to centers of employment and services.

In Phoenix, I have seen houses drop 10 and 20% in value in the outlying areas while properties are still appreciating within the cities. During slower times, I have driven through the outlying subdivisions and about 30% of the houses either had "For Sale" or "For Rent" signs in front of them. The owners could not rent or sell their houses; they were competing with the builders and with their very motivated neighbors.

QUICK REVIEW

1. Homes in outlying areas are less expensive to buy; however, it is very difficult to rent them.
2. Depending on the quantity of homes available, property values may decrease and it might be difficult to sell or rent homes on the perimeter of a large metropolitan area.

INSIGHT 30

Condos are the First to Go Down in Value, Go Down the Furthest and Stay Down the Longest.

Condominiums are the most profitable housing units that builders can build. They can build the largest number of units on an acre of ground. They can stack units on top of each other floor after floor with no additional land costs. The cities and counties love condominiums because they can collect far more property taxes without any additional expenses for streets, sewers, police and fire protection. The infrastructure is already in place, and they get to charge far more money in property taxes on the condominiums. Between the high profit potential for the builders and the phenomenal increase in property taxes for the taxing agencies, is it any wonder that the markets are always glutted with condominiums? Cities also have pressure from the Federal Government to provide as much housing as possible in their communities. Condominiums help the cities fill that void; however, not all condominiums are low priced housing units.

There are more and more luxury condos coming on the market every day. Downtown areas are being converted into luxury condominiums for people who want the convenience of living in those areas. Oceanfront properties and ski resorts can be also be very profitable locations for condos. *Just be aware, the market is nearly always saturated with condos which are not located in unique locations with unique views and a limited number of available units.*

I often have first time home buyers and even a few investors tell me that they want to buy a condominium either as their first home or as an investment property. Personally, if I had a choice between purchasing a single family home, a condominium, or renting, my first choice would be to purchase the single family home, my second choice would be to rent and my last choice would be to purchase a condominium. If I rent, I can always move out of the rental at the end of the lease period that will not be the case with a condominium that I own. I have met very few property owners that have told me that they made money from owning a condominium, but I have met hundreds that have regretted purchasing their condominium by the time they were able to get rid of it.

Excessive supplies do not create profitable markets.

INSIGHT 31

Think About What You're Buying Before Buying.

For a lot of people selecting a home to buy is not a logical process. They make their decision based on raging emotions, not on logical analysis.

I never buy a one bedroom and one bath anything. I always want at least two bedrooms and two full baths. Normally, I purchase a minimum of three bedrooms and two baths. Remember that selling begins with the selection process, so select properties that can be sold in any kind of market. If you would have a problem living in the property, you can bet someone else would have the same problem.

When prospective buyers or tenants are first examining a property, they are not looking for good features. They are looking for reasons to reject the property. Do not make it easy for them to reject your property. This applies to buyers as well as prospective tenants. You want them to fall in love with your place, not just tolerate it.

Most families today want at least two bedrooms and a room that can be used as an office for their computer work. Don't take the attitude that "it's just a rental" and you want to buy something that is small and inexpensive. Small and inexpensive can become very expensive, if it is always vacant or the tenants are constantly moving out on you. You want a property where the tenants will enjoy living and stay for several years. This minimizes your vacancy factor and time spent managing your property. When purchasing, I stay away from busy streets and intersections because someday I will want to sell or rent the property with a minimum of hassle and delays. Always consider if you would want to live in the property before you purchase it. If not, why not? Is it something that can be eliminated, corrected, or is it always going to be a big negative for the property? Do not buy someone else's headaches. You don't need them in your life; you will be able to find great properties if you take your time.

Take your time, analyze the property, and look at the good features as well as the bad. If you cannot get comfortable with the property, walk away and think about it for a few days, do not force yourself to accept something that you may not be happy owning. You are the buyer and you should be totally satisfied with the property or exercise your right to walk away from the potential purchase. Remember that you are the one that is going to be living with the property for several years, nobody else, just you and your family.

ADDITIONAL INTUITIVE CONCEPTS

QUICK REVIEW

1. Be aware that buying decisions are often based on emotions not logic.
2. Prospective buyers and renters are looking for reasons to reject a property. Keep that in mind when you purchase.
3. Minimizing vacancy saves you both money and time.

INSIGHT 32

Land Locked Cities that are Considered "High Demand or High Dollar Areas" will Appreciate in Value.

In cities that are considered exclusive areas in which to live, housing will normally continue to appreciate even when the local economy becomes soft. Buyers are willing to pay the higher prices because of the amenities associated with the city. Such locations may include an excellent school system, shopping, high income neighborhood, scenic views or high-paying employment opportunities. Housing is more expensive to purchase or rent in these cities because people want to live there. They are willing to pay a premium to obtain housing in the area.

The prices are higher because the demand for local housing is higher, but even though you pay more to purchase a property, you should see that reflected in greater appreciation on the property. When investors focus on buying inexpensive properties, they need to consider why that property is inexpensive. Why hasn't it appreciated? There will be an obvious reason if you look for it. I do not believe in shopping for cheap properties. I shop for properties that I think will maximize my rate of appreciation.

INSIGHT 33

School Reputations are Very Important.

If you target families as your primary source of tenants, you cannot ignore the reputation of the local schools. One of the primary considerations for families with school age children is the quality of the school system, and most buyers will check out the ranking of the schools. I own a couple of houses located in a school district with an excellent reputation, I appreciate the fact that the local grade school is always rated as one of the best in the state.

There is usually a waiting list of possible tenants who would like to rent one of my houses in the school district when they become vacant. My tenants have shared with me they have looked for months to find a house to rent in the area where their children would attend that grade school. I charge maximum rents, and the tenants stay for several years in my two houses because of the local school.

If you're targeting tenants that do not have children, then the reputation of the schools are irrelevant to those tenants. Just be aware that the quality of the local schools can have a huge effect on the rate of appreciation for a property. Great schools can dramatically increase the rate of return on your investment and can make it easier to rent and sell the property. This is another example of why selling begins with the purchasing of the right property in the right location.

INSIGHT 34

Never Confuse Brains with a Bull Market.

No person is smarter than the market. Never assume that you have figured out the market. The market is always changing and whatever you have been doing is not going to continue working for very long. Many people get involved in real estate during a "hot market" and just assume that the market will always be going up. That is always a false assumption and they will get burned by it, sooner or later.

As soon as you think you have the perfect system, the market is going to change. Your perfect system can turn on you and burn you financially. I am frequently asked which investment program is best. I respond that investors must stay flexible. You must change tactics as the

ADDITIONAL INTUITIVE CONCEPTS

market changes, or you will be going in the wrong direction at the wrong time. It is my job to figure out where the market is heading next. The recent past is ancient history. A similar market situation will not return for at least another five or six years, or possibly even a lifetime.

My preference is to "buy and hold" for the long haul, which should make money for you on your investments. Short term market fluctuations will not have a huge effect on your real estate holdings. When you buy for a fast "get in and get out" situation you need to be very careful about analyzing the current and immediate market situation. If you cannot sell quickly you must be able to carry the property or hold on to it for the long haul by renting it or moving into it.

It always surprises me how people wait and wait, then rush in to purchase at the very end of a bull market. Invariable they are eaten alive financially because they are buying at the top of the market, exactly when they should have been selling.

Use the market indicators and figure out where the market is in relation to the market cycles. It is not that difficult to figure out. Just put in a little time and effort. The information is readily available and it is free. Do not assume that because you have been experiencing a bull market, it will still be a bull market three months from now. You need to check and see if there is water in the pool before jumping off the diving board.

QUICK REVIEW

1. Do not assume you have figured out the market.
2. Long-term investing in real estate is safer because you have more tolerance for changes in the market.
3. Do your homework. Determine what part of a business cycle the market is in.

True vision is always twofold. It involves emotional comprehensions as well as physical perceptions.

- ROSS PARMENTOR

CHAPTER SEVEN

IMPORTANT CONTEMPLATIONS

INSIGHT 35

How to Calculate the Purchase Price for a "Fixer-up Property."

When contemplating purchasing distressed properties, you must be very careful that you do not get caught in the common trap of paying too much. In an active real estate market it is very difficult to buy property for a price that can be profitable. Always remember that at any given time period there is a limit to the market values for any neighborhood. Your final sales price must never exceed those values.

Your first step is to determine the most you can reasonably sell a property for after it is fixed up. Each neighborhood has a price range from a low to a high that housing sells and appraises for in that area. Even if you have a buyer willing to pay more than market value for the property, if the buyer is going to need financing to complete the transaction, the property must appraise for the sales price. If it does not appraise for the sales price, the property will not qualify for the loan amount that the transaction may require. The buyer and the property both must qualify for the financing; the property qualifies by appraising for at least the amount of the sales price.

I have found that if you take a normal neighborhood of homes that are over ten years old and do your regular market analysis to determine the market value of the subject property, you can add about ten percent to the value of the house if it is completely remodeled. In other words, determine the market value of a similar house in the same area and assume that they are in average condition. Then you can add about ten percent to that value. Assuming that the property will be completely remodeled, it should sell and appraise for that higher value.

Now that you have established the top end of the market value for the property, you must be able to buy the property at a discounted price. You are going to incur remodeling costs, vacancy costs, selling costs, and hopefully make a profit. Do not forget that you are going to have a couple of silent partners that are going to want their share of the profits, who will not share in the risk, work or time that will be required. The State and Federal Governments are entitled to tax your income for their share of the profits

You must be able to buy the property usually for no more than seventy percent of what it will sell for after being remodeled. You should work up a detailed estimate of what the repairs are going to cost you before making an offer to purchase. You will have the costs of several months of vacancy to cover, and then you must allow for buying and selling costs. They can take a big chunk out of your equity (normal selling costs equal about 10% of selling price).

You will find that after four or five houses, you can become very proficient at estimating the costs of repairs. You will also find that the basic costs are very close to the same no matter what condition the house is in at the time of purchase. You will need to replace the flooring, appliances, and paint, and those costs are going to be incurred on each property. Then be aware of the big-ticket items that you may have to cover such as replacing the roof, damaged foundation, heating and air conditioning, or termite damage. Such items can really hurt if you have not allowed for them in your cost estimates.

After you have purchased the property, made the repairs, and allowed for your vacancy costs, you must also allow for selling expenses, which will vary from area to area. You can calculate them as a percentage of the selling price once you have determined what is customary for your area. It will greatly reduce your costs if you can pay cash for the property and the repairs. Then you must figure out how to reduce your selling costs as much as possible. To do it right, you need to have access to large amounts of cash, since many of the properties will not qualify for financing because of their overall condition. Financing also costs money and you need to limit your total costs as much as possible.

You will find that there is a very competitive market for properties classified as "fix-ups." In fact, there are now nationwide franchises that buy distressed properties, fix them up, and then resell them. They operate with virtually unlimited amounts of cash. They have architects, accounting, and legal staff available as needed. They also purchase materials in bulk since they know most distressed properties need the same repairs. This is a very brutal business, especially if you are going to learn by trial and error. The waters are full of sharks, and you had better be prepared to swim with them.

If you are going to get involved in flipping or fixing-up and flipping, you need to understand that timing is absolutely critical. You need to buy the property at a distressed price, make your repairs and resell the property before the market makes a correction. It is very difficult to purchase homes at distressed prices in a hot market, but if you can find them, they will sell very quickly. In a slow market, it is much easier to find property to purchase, but much more difficult to resell. The real disaster occurs when buyer's pay too much in a hot market, make their repairs, and then learn the market has tanked. They have more in the property than it is worth.

Be very conservative on your repairs to the property. It is very easy to over spend while making repairs. Develop a budget up front and keep track of your expenditures as you proceed with the repairs. If you have a full time job, I do not recommend that you get involved in buying and flipping if you are going to do the repairs yourself. It is simply too time-consuming.

Cash is king when buying fix-ups, repairing and reselling. You simply cannot have too much free cash. Many properties will not qualify for financing if they are in need of serious repairs. I always tell my customers that the property must be structurally sound, and there cannot be any conditions that may create safety concerns such as bare electrical wires or missing light fixtures, if they need or want financing. The investor may need to pay cash for the property, cash for the repairs and cover vacancy costs while waiting to sell the property.

It is very important to understand that it may not be cost effective to make certain types of property improvements such as adding swimming pools and/or increasing the square footage of the living area of the dwelling. If it is a small two bedroom/ one bath house on a large lot it may greatly increase the value by adding a couple of bedrooms and a bath. However, the immediate area or subdivision should have comparable homes of the same size after the property has been increased in size. Never over-build for the neighborhood; you will lose money on the improvements.

I work with many police officers in my mortgage business, and I had an officer come into my office and ask for advice regarding some properties that he had purchased and fixed up. He and four partners had bought five properties and fixed them up just like new homes. These properties were about 30 years old and had never been up-dated, so they stripped them down to the bare walls and replaced everything in the houses. All the officers had maxed out their credit cards, used up their savings, and refinanced their cars to get cash. Now they had five vacant houses on the market.

They received a purchase contract on one of the properties for their asking price. The buyer's income and credit was excellent, but when the lender received the appraisal on the property, it appraised for about fifty thousand less than the asking price. At the appraised value, the seller's were going to lose about thirty thousand dollars on the property. At that point, he was referred to me by another police officer who thought I might be able to help.

Unfortunately, all I could do was go online and verify that the appraisal was indeed done correctly and that the value on the appraisal was correct. I completed a market evaluation on all five properties they had purchased. I asked him not to give me the purchase prices until I had completed the market evaluation on the properties. What I came up with for market values on each property plus raising the values by ten percent because of the excellent condition was less than what they had initially paid for each property. In addition, they had incurred the cost of repairs, several months of vacancy, purchasing costs, and selling costs which all together totaled far more than the market value of the properties.

My suggestion was they should hold onto the properties and rent them until they could sell them for enough to cover their costs. He felt that was not possible since the properties would not rent for near enough to cover the house payments. They could not afford to carry the monthly payments on their outstanding credit card balances.

I am telling you this because this is not an unusual situation; it happens often. Let's see if we can learn anything from this tragic situation. First, they used a part-time REALTOR® and loan officer who had no experience with investment properties. The REALTOR® was one of the partners, a full-time police officer and part-time REALTOR®. Second, they did not evaluate the market conditions, and at the time interest rates were very high. Third, they did not do a market evaluation of the properties and determine what the top sales prices were in the area. Fourth, they spent way too much money on the repairs, even though they did most of the work themselves. Fifth, they did not have adequate capital or experience to take on five properties at one time. Sixth they did not have a back-up plan in case the properties did not sell for the amount they needed.

They put a tremendous amount of work on the properties and spent every dime that they could scrape up between themselves. What they did not do was take some time and learn about the market and come up with a workable plan before they dove into troubled waters. I wished they had taken the time to talk to me before they had. I am sure that all five of them filed bankruptcy because of the financial disaster they created for themselves.

IMPORTANT CONTEMPLATIONS

QUICK REVIEW

1. Make sure you have a detailed and accurate estimate of all repair costs involved.
2. "Fix-up" properties are in demand and you will be competing with large companies that will try to purchase them.
3. Having large amounts of cash will save you money on purchases and repairs.
4. Not doing the necessary research can lead to a financial disaster.

The only man that makes no mistakes is the man who never does anything.

- ELEANOR ROOSEVELT

INSIGHT 36

Have Several Systems for Finding and Buying Properties.

You need to have more than one system for purchasing properties that work for you and your schedule. You do not need to be an expert in all procedures, and you should not try to use all of the various procedures for your purchases. Find a few that will work with your schedule, your expertise, and your budget. You do not want to try and purchase every property that is for sale. You can make amazing amounts of money from just one great purchase per year.

Buying Systems that Work

1. Start first with an owner-occupied property. This should be the first property that you purchase. It will be the easiest to finance and the simplest to manage. Consider moving after two years and using part of the equity from your first home to purchase a second owner occupied home. The first home you purchased then becomes your first rental property.
2. Buy a fix–up house, fix it up, and rent it or move into it. Buy it at a discount of about 30% or do not buy it. Work with local REALTORS® who have experience with investment properties. Let them know what type of properties you are interested in purchasing.
3. Bank foreclosures can be an excellent source of properties. Make sure that you verify the property values in the immediate area. Do not overpay for the property, and remember that you are buying it in "as-is condition." Check the web sites that show local foreclosure properties, and your REALTOR® should be able to help you by finding bank properties listed for sale.
4. New homes can be an excellent source for investment properties. When the real estate market slows, builders become very motivated seller's. I have bought most of my properties from new home builders. I try to buy when a sub-division first becomes available for sale before the builder raises the prices of the homes. A few words of warning are appropriate at this time. A new house will require considerable cash investment after you own it to make it livable. The property may not appreciate to its full potential until after the builder completes the sub-division. If you should need to sell before the tract is completed you will be competing with the builder and other seller's in the sub-division.
5. My favorite way to buy is to find a house that is vacant and has been on the market for several months. That property will probably be owned by a very motivated seller. Newspaper ads of properties for sale by the owners can be a good source for properties. You must be financially prepared to move immediately on the property. I have found that if the house is vacant and the owner has moved out of state, it can be a very exciting opportunity.
6. Relocation companies for major companies nearly always have properties for sale and most of them are in very good condition. You may be able to find some excellent properties at great prices.

IMPORTANT CONTEMPLATIONS

7. Always be alert for a possible buying opportunity you may come across at any time during your normal activities. They are out there for the person who is prepared to recognize them and has the resources to move on them.

INSIGHT 37

How to Make Money in a "No-Growth Economy."

There are parts of this country where growth simply does not exist. In fact, the very centers of the U.S. and several northern states have very slow growth rates. In some counties in those areas, the population is actually declining. I have a customer that retired as a fireman in Minnesota. He owns about thirty properties in several different cities in the state. He buys houses for fifteen thousand to thirty thousand dollars per house and rents them for five hundred to eight hundred dollars per month.

He spends the summers in Minnesota making repairs and renting the properties and then returns to Phoenix for the winter. If he does not have the houses rented by the end of September, they will sit vacant all winter and will not rent until the following summer. He does not expect any appreciation, but he does have substantial cash flow from the properties. His purchase prices are so low he gets plenty of positive cash flow from the houses even if he does not get them all rented.

He typically pays cash for the houses at the time of purchase or has the seller carry the financing with a very small down payment. Typically, the seller's are more than willing to carry the financing because the houses have been on the market for a long time or were part of an estate. He now purchases real estate in Phoenix, but he still has substantial positive cash flow from the properties in Minnesota. He gets appreciation on his properties in Phoenix and cash flow on the other properties, not a bad combination for someone that wants to spend their summers in Minnesota and winters in Phoenix.

I have a son, Robert, who lives in a small town in Kansas and has a slightly different wrinkle to his game plan. He obtained a line of credit with a local bank and uses that line of credit to purchase houses that have been repossessed by the bank. Repossessed property is called REO property (real estate owned), and banks must sell the property to get as much of their money back as they can. He buys the houses for forty to sixty thousand dollars each, pays for the house, and makes any necessary repairs with the line of credit. Then he either resells the house or refinances it and keeps it as investment property. He seems to do very well at it and there seem to be a steady supply of houses that the banks need to move.

To me this is kind of like buying himself a job, but if that is what he wants to do, more power to him. I am not excited about living in a small town, but for people who do live there or would like, this might be a way for them to make a very good living. They should be willing to manage the property and perform most of the maintenance work themselves.

A property must either appreciate, generate positive cash flow, or both, or I am not going to be interested in owning it. Yes, I need a place to live, but I can find a place to live that will also appreciate in value while I am living there.

QUICK REVIEW

1. Have several systems for finding properties that you may want to purchase.
2. Start with an owner-occupied home.
3. Consider fix-up homes, bank foreclosures, a new home, or a relocation home. Constantly be alert for potential buying opportunities.

Money doesn't always bring happiness. People with $10 million are no happier than people with $9 million.

- HOBERT BROWN

IMPORTANT CONTEMPLATIONS

INSIGHT 38

Pricing for a fast and profitable sale.

Always remember that the preparation for the sale of a property begins before the purchase. Buy the type of housing in a location that will continue to appreciate in value over time. Buy in areas in which employment is increasing and great amenities either exist or will be built in the immediate future. It is important to buy property where people want to live, now and in the future.

Let's assume that we have a property and are preparing to place it on the market. You need to understand the fundamentals that create demand and value for real estate.

1. *Location* is the first fundamental which increases or decreases value for all real estate. It is the one item that can not be changed or modified. Most factors can be changed but it may cost time and money. It is very important that a property is not located near a busy street, intersection, or near overhead power lines. Negative factors like these can lower the property values by 10 to 15%. Such factors can also make it extremely difficult to sell or rent the property without drastically reducing the price in a slow market.
2. *Market Conditions.* The markets can usually be divided up into three distinctly different types. The "seller's market" (hot market) has a shortage of inventory for sale and a surplus of buyer's wanting to buy. The buyer's bid up the price of houses because the demand is greater than the available supply of homes.
A "normal market" has a fairly good balance between demand and supply, and the two forces are in approximate equilibrium. In a normal market houses normally appreciate at about 2-3% higher than the rate of inflation.
A "buyer's market" (slow market) has a surplus of seller's or homes on the market versus the number of available buyer's. In this type of market, housing prices will actually be declining.
3. *Market Interest Rates.* As interest rates increase, property values tend to decrease and salability declines dramatically. As interest rates decline, demand for real estate increases drastically and property values start increasing. It is important to be aware

of interest rates and understand which direction the local economy is headed, and why.
4. *Price.* This is the second fundamental of real estate which increases or decreases the demand for the property. I will explain why it was not listed in second place in a few paragraphs. As with nearly all products, as the price increases, the demand decreases. Fewer buyer's will be able or willing to buy at the higher prices. Overpricing your property will simply help sell your neighbor's house; it makes theirs look like a better value for the money.
5. *Financing Terms* can dramatically affect the salability of a property in a slow market. In the past, I have offered to help pay some of the buyer's closing cost expenses when negotiating for the sale of a property. This decreases the amount of cash that the buyer needs to close the escrow.
6. *Property condition.* Excellent property condition can somewhat offset higher prices and greatly speed up the selling process. When potential buyer's first look at a property, they are not looking for reasons to buy that property, they are looking for reasons to reject it. That is why first impressions are extremely important, you want the buyer's to immediately "fall in love" with the property not just think "its o.k., this could work."

It is important to understand all six of the fundamentals of value and how they affect the salability of homes. Only the last three of them can be modified or changed by you; those are the ones that I listed last and the ones that you must focus on as a seller. The first three factors will be beyond your control at the time of marketing. That is why a great location at the time of purchase is so very important. Location cannot be changed. You cannot change slow market conditions and you will have no control over interest rates. That is why I believe it is extremely important to try and time your buying and selling based upon market conditions. You can choose to buy in slow markets and sell in hot markets.

Have you ever wondered what conditions creates a seller's' market versus the other kind of markets? Normally a seller's' market is created when interest rates have been at historically low rates for several years. These low rates stimulate the economy and create many new jobs, especially in the construction industry. The construction industry affects nearly all segments of our economy, creating what is called a huge "income multiplier" in the local economy. Money spent on construction is dispersed throughout the economy, and it generates jobs and income for construction, engineering, financial services, real estate, materials, government services, etc.

Eventually, these additional jobs and increases in income increase the demand for local housing and just about every other product or service in our society. Then bad things begin to happen. Everything, including houses, begins to increase in price at a higher rate than people's income; these price increases are called inflation. If the Federal Reserve lowers interest rates, those new rates create a huge demand for real estate which in turn increases property appreciation. Eventually, housing becomes more expensive than people can afford to pay.

As a seller, it is hard to go wrong in a seller's' market. Property values are appreciating and potential buyer's are desperate to buy. The biggest concerns the seller's have is selling before the property values have peaked. This really should not be a big concern for the seller. It is hard to say a seller made a mistake by selling early if they made a substantial profit on the transaction. The biggest mistake I see are seller's holding on too long, and then the hot market passes them by before they sell.

The transition from a "seller's' market," to a "buyer's' market," happens very quickly and it is not a slow transition, it happens in a very short time period. What causes the market to change so quickly? Normally, market change is engineered by the Federal Reserve System. Once the Fed decides to slow the economy down, they act very firmly and quickly. How do they accomplish this transition? They raise short term interest rates and since housing is a capital intensive industry, the increase in interest rates along with the recent high levels of appreciation have a devastating affect on the local housing industry. It immediately deflates existing home sales as well as new home sales.

In a seller's market, the seller only needs to be concerned about the price and the condition of the property. There will not be any financing incentives offered, and the condition of the property is not nearly as important as in a buyer's market. In a seller's market the seller may be able to ask and get 10 -15% above the actual market value for their property, and may get 5 to 10 offers at the same time from various buyer's. They may create a bidding war for the property. This is not a healthy market and it will come to an abrupt end, because the Feds will terminate this type of market condition.

In a *normal market*, the markets are in balance, and the number of homes for sale is enough to supply the housing needs for the active buyer's. In this type of market, the homes will be appreciating at 2-3% above the rate of inflation, and the rate of inflation will be 2% or less per annum. Housing appreciates at 2-3% above the rate of inflation simply because the costs of land, labor and materials continually increase each year. In a normal market, as a seller, you probably need only to be concerned about correct pricing and the condition of your property. The market is functioning correctly, and the seller normally does not need to provide financing incentives for the buyer's. This is a healthy market and should continue for several years as long as new jobs are being created in the local economy.

In a *"buyer's market,"* (slow market), many people get hurt financially. There is a surplus of homes on the market, and a shortage of buyer's. Few are buying and property values are declining; seller's are confused, nervous or even desperate to sell. They cannot get anyone to even preview their home, let alone make an offer on it. Why is the market so slow, what has happened, where are the buyer's, why are the houses declining in value? These are very good questions, and I believe I can help answer them for you.

During a seller's market (hot market) the prices of homes can go up 10 to 50% per year for several years in row. Remember, during a seller's market you will always have very low interest rates to finance the purchase of houses. Even with houses appreciating at very fast rates more buyer's will be able to afford the higher prices because the lower interests rates help keep their payments low. The lenders will provide new loan products that will help keep the monthly payments as low as possible such as interest only, negative amortization, and adjustable rates. Now, they have extended the length of the loans from 30 years to 40 and 50 years, all in an attempt to keep the monthly payments more affordable for the borrowers.

Sooner or later, the Fed decides everyone is having too much fun and the party is getting out of hand. They will slam on the brakes by increasing interest rates. This increase in rates, along with the accumulated appreciation of several years, simply makes the prices of housing too high for buyer's. *A seller's market is always followed by a buyer's market.* The increase in interest rates combined with the property appreciation will always create this market situation. Buyer's markets will normally last about three years after the market peaks during the seller's market. The buyer's market will be followed by a normal market that should last 10 to 15 years, as long as there is new job creation in the local market.

Now, let's discuss selling in a buyer's market, which is very difficult to do. It is important to remember that a seller's market and a buyer's market are not healthy markets and each should only last for 2 to 3 years in a growing local economy. The normal market is a healthy market and should last for 10-15 years in a growing economy.

Try to avoid selling in a buyer's market as much as possible. You are going to leave a lot of money on the table while trying to sell. It is going to be a very frustrating and expensive experience for you. Look for alternatives to selling until the market corrects itself. It may only take a few months. Remember that May through August is the peak selling months. If your property does not sell during those months you can figure it won't sell until the following April.

Watch interest rates. Are they going up, or declining? If they are increasing, the market will be slowing down. If they are decreasing, the market will be improving. Do not fight the markets. Work with them, not against them, because you will lose money in the long run if you fight them.

I have noticed that interest rates have often peaked in the middle of June, after which they decline and bottom out in the November through January time periods. If I decide that I want to refinance a property I always try to do so in November and December because that is usually when the rates are at their lowest during a calendar year.

Assume you have accepted a new job, or got married, or divorced, or retired, or had more children. Due to the changes in your life you must sell and sell quickly in a very slow market. How do you handle it?

The important thing you need to understand if you are selling in a buyer's market is that your house has declined in value. It is not worth today what it was worth a few months before. That's life. Face reality and deal with it—the values of all products move up and down depending upon the market demand and availability for that product at any given time.

Remember that you probably purchased your property for much less than you're trying to sell it for and may not have made any major improvements to the property. If the property has doubled or tripled in value since you purchased it, are you really getting hurt by the current market conditions? If you recently purchased the property, you are probably going to take a loss on the sale. The only guarantees in life are death and taxes. You can improve your odds with proper planning and preparation. Buy in slow markets and sell in hot markets and do not get greedy in a hot market. Take advantage of it.

When marketing your property, understand how real estate agents and individual buyer's decide which properties to preview and which ones to ignore. They nearly always look for properties in certain geographic neighborhoods, with certain features and prices. They decide on a square footage, bedrooms, baths, garage, size, schools, churches, shopping, and price range. If your house is priced above their targeted price range, they are not even going to preview it. If you are not getting any showings of your house, it is overpriced for the current market conditions. The price needs to be dramatically reduced or you need to remove the property from the market. If you are getting showings but no offers, something is still wrong. You need to get serious about the condition of the property. Does it show well? Is there too much furniture? Does it need new carpets or paint? Have you had your house "professionally staged" for showing? If not, you should consider it. How does your house show compared with new home models in the area? If you have not looked at any model homes for several years, you should. If you are convinced that your house shows as it should, you need to reduce the price to the point where you are slightly below the current market values for similar houses. Current market values mean comparable homes that have sold and closed within the last 4 to 6 months, not the last 6 to 12 months. Remember that values are dropping. If your house is overpriced, the agents will simply use your house to sell other houses in the immediate area. If houses in your area are selling and you are not getting offers, you are overpriced for the market, for the condition of your property, or for its location. If none of the houses are selling in your area, everyone is overpriced for the current market conditions. This situation happens a lot in a declining market.

In a buyer's market there are usually vacant houses sitting on the market that are owned by some very motivated seller's. You are competing with these seller's who have no choice; they must sell or risk losing their houses in foreclosure, which is what will happen to many of them. When I am shopping for property in a buyer's market, I do not even consider occupied houses. I only preview vacant houses because I know the seller's are motivated and must get out as quickly as possible.

I am not looking for that "perfect dream home." I am only looking for a fantastic buy on a nice house in a great area, and I find them. In a seller's market you can price your property 5 – 10% above market, in a normal market it should be priced within 5% of market value. In a buyer's market it should be priced slightly lower than current market values. Please note that market values and asking prices are not the same thing. Market values are determined by closed transactions of similar properties that have closed within the last 6 months.

Respect all offers that you may receive from prospective buyer's. I am amazed at how many people get downright insulted when they are presented with an offer lower than what they are asking for their property. I tell everyone that there is no such thing as bad offer. Some offers are just better than others and any offer can be countered. Control your emotions, and make sound business decisions when responding to a live offer. Counter the offer in a way which will benefit you. Do not ignore a valid offer and refuse to even counter it; that is just being stupid.

Try to work with the buyer to learn if they are serious, or just testing the waters. Maybe they do not have any experience in making offers, or they may not understand their financing options. It may benefit both of you to try to communicate with each other and determine what each party is trying to accomplish. If both parties control their emotions and work together, it works, I promise. Realize if you receive an offer and counter it, and the counter offer is not accepted, you just bought your property back for the amount of the original offer.

The correct pricing of your property in a buyer's market is going to be one of the toughest decisions you will ever make. Be realistic, the values are declining and will continue to decline for 2 to 3 years after the market peaked. If you live in an area where employment is decreasing, the market may not improve for several years or even decades.

A buyer's market is not a time to be selling, but it is a wonderful time to be aggressively buying in a growing local economy. The slow market will not last long, declining interest rates will be just around the corner and you will be back into a normal market. In a slow market, I buy excellent properties 20 to 25% below current market values and when the market corrects itself (Fed drop rates), I get downright excited. You will also get excited if you understand the concept that timing is everything. *Buy in a slow market and sell in a hot market.* It works for me and it will work for you.

QUICK REVIEW

1. Low interest rates increase economic activity which increases the demand for housing. This increased demand for housing increases the prices of housing, as well as every product and service in our economy. This demand stimulates inflation which will continue to increase as demand continues to increase. This increase in inflation forces the Fed to step in and raise interest rates to keep inflation at 2%, or less.
2. As interest rates increase the seller's market very quickly becomes a buyer's market (characterized by decreases in sales and property values). As the economy starts slowing down and the rate of inflation drops below 2%, the Fed will slowly start to decrease interest rates which will begin to stimulate the housing markets and the rest of the economy. This will create a more healthy normal housing market that should last for several years during which housing should appreciate at 2-3% above the rate of inflation.
3. In a seller's market, pricing your property correctly, not getting greedy, and selling before the market peaks are excellent strategies.
4. In a normal market, pricing and condition of the property are extremely important.
5. Try not to sell in a buyer's market, but if you must, price your property lower than comparable homes, stage your property, consider every offer, and be aware of the responses you receive and adjust the price accordingly.
6. Of the six factors that determine value you will only be able to control three of those factors: price, condition, and financing terms.
7. Market conditions vary during business cycles, and interest rates vary in cycles that are typically five to six years long.

IMPORTANT CONTEMPLATIONS

INSIGHT 39

Property Management can Make or Break You.

The ultimate success of your investment program will depend upon how well you manage your properties and select your tenants. I cannot overstress how important management is in maximizing your return. *I operate on the 20/20/60 rule; 20% of your success will depend on how well you bought the asset, 20% on the selling, and 60% on the management of the property.* Management can be an extremely horrible experience for someone who does not handle it correctly and most first-time investors do a questionable job of managing their properties. It is not fun to get sued, go to court and find out that the judge has absolutely no sympathy for your cause.

If you use common sense and follow the law to the letter, you should not have any major problems. *One of your first investments should be a current copy of your state's Landlord/Tenant Laws. Read it and understand it.* Realize that it is the law in your state and must be followed. Ignorance of the law will get you in serious financial and legal problems. It is your responsibility to know the appropriate laws.

It is easy to manage property correctly and get great tenants who can become your friends for life. I have done it many times, and I appreciate the friendships I have developed with many of my tenants over the years. If you do not have the desire or ability to manage your own property, you should consider hiring an experienced property manager to manage your rentals. Good property managers can be difficult to locate and will require some research on your part. It is well worth the time and effort that it will take to find an excellent property manager. They are out there and willing to help you.

I manage my properties myself, and I can only recall one family that I had to evict over the years. My goal is to rent good properties to wonderful families and we have always been able to resolve any problems that may arise. I like my tenants, we are friends, and I would not want to have it any other way. It certainly is not a requirement, and I know that most landlords do not even know their tenants. That is not the way I choose to do business. When I get a good buy on a nice property, I often lease the property with an "option to buy" to a qualified tenant. I will lease it for a minimum of fourteen months before the tenant can purchase the property and I give the tenants three or four years to complete the transaction. I want to own the property for more than one year to take advantage of long term capital gains tax rates. When the tenants are ready to complete the purchase, I will credit them $200.00 for each month they rented the property. That credit goes towards their closing costs and/or down payment. *I agree to sell them the property for a minimum amount stated in the option or the appraised value, whichever is the highest at the time of purchase.*

This creates an unofficial partnership between me and the tenants. I have a great tenant who will take care of the property, and it helps the tenants to generate cash for the purchase of the property at a future date. I really do like helping people purchase their first home, and this system works well for both of us.

Selling a property begins with the purchase of the property and renting a property begins with the purchase of the property. Find good properties where families will want to live and the property will appeal to the kind of people you want as tenants. Buy properties in rough neighborhoods, and you are going to get rough tenants because no one else will live there.

Advertising

After you have purchased a nice property you need to find a great tenant. I advertise in the local Sunday newspaper and on a couple of rental websites to find my tenants. Typically, my ad is about three lines long. I start by giving the general location, the square footage, number of bedrooms and baths, the monthly rent and a phone number. As the prospective tenants call, I give them the exact address and ask them to drive-by to see if they are interested in seeing the rest of the house. If they call back, I will then make an appointment to show them the house. This saves me time because I am not scheduling appointments with people who are not interested in the property.

Credit

If after seeing the house the prospective tenants want to rent it, I ask them to complete a rental application indicating their last two years of employment and residency. I tell them that I will need to run a current credit report on them. If they have a problem with the credit report, we are finished. I don't want to rent to people who are not financially stable. If they are comfortable with me running their credit report, it will probably turn out to show fairly good credit. Most tenants do not have perfect credit. If they did, they would most likely be homeowners.

I do not expect perfect credit, but I do want to see that they pay their bills on time, especially their rent and/or past house payments. Your lender should be willing to run the applicant's credit report for you for a small fee. You want a tri-merged credit report on each adult that is going to occupy the premises along with their FICO scores. They should have a FICO score of 600 or higher.

If you see several unpaid collections or judgments, especially judgments from previous landlords or apartment complexes, you do not want them as tenants. *You must always remember that you are not a welfare agency, and you cannot let their financial problems become your financial problems.* If they do not have adequate good credit, send them on down the road. You do not want to be wasting your time and money on tenants who are not going to pay the rent.

If they have not paid other creditors, they will not pay you. I qualify them just like I qualify borrowers who want to borrow money to purchase a house. That starts with the borrower's credit report, and they either have good credit or they do not. I can get borrowers approved for a loan to buy a house without a property appraisal, no money down, even no job or income. I cannot get any loan for a borrower without a decent credit report and credit scores. I do not know of a loan that is available without an acceptable credit report on the borrower. This should give you an idea of how important a perspective tenant's credit should be to you.

Residency

Assuming that they have decent credit, I believe it is important to know how long they have lived at each address. A lot of people do not stay at the same address very long. They tend to move just about ever year, or even sooner. I want tenants who have stayed at the same address for several years, either as tenants or property owners. Fewer turnovers save you time and money. Families who have a history of staying at the same addresses for a long time will stay at your property for several years. Tenants either like to move often or they hate moving with a passion. I know, because I hate moving with a passion and can identify with that type of customer.

Income

The second thing I look for is a stable income. It's similar to moving, they either stay at the same job, or they bounce around from job to job. I want as much stability in their employment as I can possibly get. What is the most stable form of employment or should I say stable form of income? Retirement is very stable, how many people give up retirement income?

Calculate their income ratio. Their contractual obligations such as car payments, credit cards, student loans, child support payments and the rent payment should not exceed 40% of their combined gross income. If their ratio is much higher than 40%, they may not be able to afford the monthly rent payment. Face up to it and deal with it at that time, not after they have moved into your property.

Retirees may go back to work, but normally it is part time work to keep themselves from going crazy. I love renting to retirees. They stay in the property, they take care of it, they pay their rent on time, and they are usually wonderful people. I also hire them to take care of the landscaping and perform maintenance work on my properties. They become my friends and I value their friendship and their help with the properties.

After you have found a prospective tenant, you need to have a "fair and reasonable lease." Get the terms of the lease in writing. It cannot be so one-sided that everything in the lease is in the landlord's favor or a judge will simply declare the contract null and unenforceable. It must be fair to both parties, must be in writing, must be signed and dated by both parties. Your REALTOR® should be able to help you with a blank lease which will be suitable for the landlord/tenant laws in your state.

Set up a file for each property and place the application, credit report and lease in the appropriate file. Two or three years down the road, you will need to be able to refer back to the lease to see what the two parties had agreed to at the time. I guarantee you it will happen. I am always referring back to the leases to see what we had agreed to years before. I normally lease a property for one or two years at a time depending on what the tenant wants. I never lease for less than a year. After the lease period is up, I usually do not extend the lease on an annual basis, unless the tenant requests it. By law in Arizona, once the lease period is up the lease becomes a month-to-month tenancy, unless both parties agree in writing to a new lease period.

You can get a complete copy of the act from your state's Attorney General's Office, or you can go online to **www.lectlaw.com/files/lat03.htm**. Each state will have its own version of the Landlord/Tenant Laws. It is your responsibility to make sure that you are following the law according to your specific state.

I never give the tenants possession of the property until they have paid all of the rent and security deposits with a cashier's check. I never accept cash from the tenant, I will explain why later. In Arizona the security deposits are limited by law to one and a half months rent. I always charge the first months rent plus a one thousand dollar refundable deposit. I intentionally keep my required deposits low because I want as many tenants as possible to apply to rent the property. I can then choose the most qualified tenant out of several applicants.

I never take a partial payment of rent or deposits up front with a promise that the rest will be paid at some future date. If the tenant cannot come up with all of the required rent and deposits up front do you really want them in your property? If you do accept a partial payment I can just about assure you that you will never get the rest of the money.

One of the worst things that a landlord can do is agree to rent their property to the first person who pulls out a fist full of cash and says that they want the house. If you go along with this ploy, I can assure you that you will never get another dime out of the tenants. Just explain to the tenants that your company has policies that you must follow, and you are not allowed to accept cash.

Offer them an application and explain that you must have an application and a copy of their current credit report before any commitment can be made. At this point in time, they will either agree to complete the application or they will be running out the door. If they want to run, by all means let them run. You do not want them in your house! *There is one thing far worse than a vacant house and that is a house with a bad tenant.*

Maintain, maintain, and maintain the property to keep your tenants happy and prevent any damage to your property or harm to the tenants because of poor maintenance. The following points need to be followed each time.

QUICK REVIEW

1. Always require a completed, dated, and signed rental application. The application should include name, social security number, and place of employment, income, and current landlord information.
2. Always run a tri-merged credit report on all adult tenants and make sure you understand any derogatory issues on their report.
3. Calculate the prospective tenant's income ratio. Total monthly contractual obligations should not exceed 40% of combined monthly gross income.
4. Do a walk through and inspect the property with the tenants and have them sign the inspection report before signing a lease. Make note of any deficiencies in the property and have them fixed before the tenants take possession. Also, take photos of the property.
5. Get a signed and dated lease before giving them possession of the property. All adults who are going to live in the property must sign the lease, and make sure the tenants receive a signed copy of the lease. A lease is required by the Statute of Frauds if the rental period is for twelve months, or more.
6. In the 1970's, the Uniform Residential Landlord and Tenant Act became law in several states. The purpose of the act was to put the relationship between the landlord and the tenant on a somewhat level playing field. It also clearly defines what is required of the landlord and of the tenant and lets the landlords know exactly how to deal with various situations.
7. Warning! Be very careful about accepting a partial payment of the rent; you may not be able to proceed with an eviction until the following month. Carefully document any partial payments and clarify in writing when any additional payments are to be paid.
8. If you decide to keep part or all of the tenant's deposit, you must be able to account for all of the money. If the tenant has damaged the property, take photos of the damage and be able to provide receipts for the repairs.

IMPORTANT CONTEMPLATIONS

9. If in doubt about anything relating to a lease, get legal advice before proceeding in a direction which you may create legal problems for yourself.
10. It is illegal for a landlord to refuse to rent to or refuse to allow a tenant with a disability to modify the property at the tenant's expense so that they can enjoy the use of the property. If you encounter this situation, you should consult with a real estate attorney before proceeding with any modifications.

INSIGHT 40

Know your Local and State Government Regulations Regarding Residential Rentals.

Again, each state has laws and regulations regarding residential rental properties, and you as an investor must know and understand the applicable laws which pertain to your properties. You need a current copy of your state's landlord/tenant laws. Read, understand, and follow them. No exceptions. You may very well be subject to city and county laws in addition to the state laws. There are areas with very strict rent controls and they can have a huge effect on the value of your property. If you have any doubts about what you're doing, consult with an attorney before taking any action. I would recommend that you consult with an attorney who specializes in Real Estate Law. If you need to evict a tenant, there are lawyers who specialize in that service and they are very inexpensive. There are legal procedures for evicting a tenant which must be followed to the letter of the law. Do not ever try going around the legal processes.

The landlord has specific legal obligations to a tenant. His first is to deliver possession of the property to the tenant on the date specified in the lease. The second obligation is to maintain the property in a fit and habitable condition. This includes items such as heating, air conditioning, maintenance repairs, running water, and hot water.

If the property has a swimming pool, you must have adequate protection for the tenants. Fencing is absolutely required, along with warning signs. I personally do not own a rental property with a swimming pool; I just do not want the liability. If someone drowns in one of your pools, you know that some lawyer will be coming after everything that you own. I have known investors who did everything according to the law regarding a swimming pool and they went bankrupt defending themselves in court. There is such a thing in life known as "winning the battle and losing the war."

You must disclose any hazardous condition regarding the property to the tenants. Items like lead-based paint, asbestos, mold, and any other hazardous condition must be disclosed in writing and dealt with to make the property safe. The landlord must provide a safe environment for the tenant that is the law.

The tenants are entitled to "Peaceful and Quiet Enjoyment of the Premises." That also is the law. You may not disturb the tenants or let other tenants disturb them. They are entitled to the use and enjoyment of the property as long as the lease is in effect. The landlord may not enter the property without proper legal notice as required by various state laws. The landlord does have the right to enter in case of an emergency such as fire, flooding, electrical problems or some other similar emergency.

In Arizona, the landlord must give the tenant at least a forty-eight hour notice before entering the property, except in an emergency situation. Each state has its own legal requirements regarding the amount of advance notice the tenant must receive. There are excellent books available in bookstores that are state specific and cover the various legal requirements between a landlord and a tenant. *I would recommend that you purchase a book that covers your specific state requirements and a current copy of your local landlord/tenant laws.*

QUICK REVIEW

1. Get a signed and dated application from each adult who is going to occupy the premises.
2. Run a current copy of each applicant's credit report. Evaluate the credit very carefully.
3. Calculate their debt ratio by dividing their combined contractual monthly debts (including the rent) by their monthly income; the ratio should not exceed 40% of their combined monthly income.
4. Inspect the premises with the tenants and have them sign the inspection report.
5. Take photos of the property.
6. All adult parties must sign and date the lease agreement.
7. All adult parties must receive a signed and dated copy of the lease.
8. Do not accept cash, only money orders or cashier's checks for the full amount due.
9. After receiving all required monies, give the tenants two sets of keys and two garage door openers.
10. Keep accurate and complete files on each property. You will need to refer back to them when questions may arise.
11. Maintain the property in a safe and functional manner.
12. Conduct a property inspection with the tenant after they move out and get keys and garage door openers from the tenants.
13. If necessary, take photos of damaged property.
14. Keep copies of receipts for any necessary repairs.
15. Account for all deposits.
16. Change the locks on doors and get new keys. Do not forget to the change the codes on garage door openers.
17. Always have a current copy of your state's landlords/tenant laws.

Ignorance of the law is no excuse.

INSIGHT 41

Holding Title to Property—I Do Not Own Anything.

You should consult with your Attorney and your CPA with respect to how you should hold title to your properties. I tell everyone that I do not own anything of value; I do not have title in my name on any of my properties. I am going to explain what I do, and why, but you need to consult with your experts about what *you* should do and why.

I have a Revocable Family Living Trust and within that trust is an Education Trust. The Education Trust holds title to a Limited Liability Company, that LLC holds title to two Partnerships. Those two partnerships each currently hold title to one half of the various properties. Yes, it was complicated to set this entire thing up, but I think it is necessary in today's society. Once it was completed, it has not been difficult to keep track of everything.

Let's take it a step at a time. The advantage of the Revocable Living Trust is that it can be changed or dissolved at anytime by the parties who originated the trust. We can add properties, refinance, or sell properties. The trust gives me the same options as owning the properties in my own name. The biggest advantage is that it allows you to avoid probate in case something happens to the grantors. If my wife and I pass away, we do not own the properties; they are owned by the trust. The trust will continue on according to the wishes of the original grantors.

The Limited Liability Company that is owned by the trust provides limited liability which the trust by itself does not provide. Liability is limited to the value of the property owned by the LLC. This LLC owns two partnerships which actually hold title to the various properties. The cost of establishing the trust and the various partnerships was not overly expensive; I just look at it as part of the cost of doing business.

Remember, you want to take a conservative approach to your investment program and make it as sound and secure as possible. You do not have to use this concept. You can simply take title to the properties in your own name. However, if you are involved in an automobile accident or someone gets injured on one of your properties, you may (will) be sued. The LLC protects some of your assets. Wouldn't it just be prudent good business to protect your assets as much as possible?

If you have a will, you may be satisfied with your estate planning, but do you know that an

IMPORTANT CONTEMPLATIONS

estate that is only covered with a will must go through probate? The national average costs of probate proceedings are approximately twenty eight percent of the estate. Probate can involve large amounts of money, loss of privacy, aggravation, and can take one to two years to finish the probate. A Revocable Family Trust avoids the hassle and costs of probate proceedings. You can hold title to real estate in your name, a trust, a corporation, a partnership or an LLC. *Check with your attorney about how you should hold title to your property. This is not the time to scrimp on getting good legal advice.*

If you are considering a change in your estate, you should check with a company that specializes in estate planning. It is not expensive to have everything organized as you would want it in case something happens to you and your spouse. Planning ahead can avoid expense, time and hard feelings after you have moved on to the "happy hunting grounds." If it is worth doing, it should be done correctly. It is not a question of "if," but "when" you will need estate planning.

QUICK REVIEW

1. Plan ahead, so transferring your assets to the next generation saves them time, money, and hassle.
2. Get good advice about protecting your assets.
3. Consider Revocable Family Trusts, LLCs, and partnerships as tools to protect assets.

Everybody's got to die sometime. That's life.

— ARCHIE BUNKER

INSIGHT 42

Good Insurance Coverage Protects your Assets.

Bad things happen; plan for them as best as you can. You must have adequate insurance to stay in business. Real estate is a business and you need to run it like a business. Do not skimp on insurance coverage or you will regret it down the road, when it is too late to make changes. Lenders will always require enough coverage to cover the loan amounts of any mortgages. In addition, you need coverage for items like rent loss. If the property is destroyed, the insurance coverage will cover the costs to rebuild, but the borrower will still be liable for the house payments. Since the house is destroyed, the owner will not be collecting rents from a tenant because the tenant was forced to move. Rent loss coverage will cover the amount of rent that the tenant would have been paying before the property improvements were damaged or destroyed. It typically takes about a year before an insurance company completes major repairs to a house.

It is very important to understand that most insurance policies can be declared "null and void" if a house sits vacant for more than 30 days. Even if you have paid the full year's policy in advance, if that property is vacant more than 30 days you may not have insurance coverage. If you file a major claim against the policy, the insurance inspector will check to see if the property has been occupied. They will talk to neighbors, check out a copy of the listing if the property is for sale and verify with the utility companies that the utilities are connected and being utilized. If the insurance adjustor determines that the property has been vacant for more than 30 days, they may deny the claim. If you have a swimming pool on the property you will need pool coverage. Just realize that if someone drowns in that pool someone is going to be after you for everything that you own or may ever own.

I have always carried a blanket liability policy of one million dollars of coverage. It covers all of my properties and automobiles. The policy costs $150.00 per year plus $15.00 per year for each property and automobile. I have never had a claim filed against me and I hope I never do, but I sleep better at night knowing that I have the policy.

Many people have learned the hard way that their regular homeowners' policy does not cover flood damage. If your property is in a flood zone, you need flood insurance in addition to your regular homeowner's policy. Buying property next to the coast and not having flood insurance is absolutely ridiculous to me. That is similar to buying a second home located in a forest and not having adequate fire insurance coverage.

Earthquake coverage is also a necessity in an area that is prone to earthquakes. We cannot prevent natural disasters from happening, but we can cover our assets as best as possible. Personally, I do not view most natural disasters as disasters; it is nature simply doing what it has been doing since the earth was created.

Like all contracts, insurance coverage should not be taken lightly. It is important and can keep you in business should you incur a major loss. It is simply a cost of doing business. Pay for it as you go or risk sudden financial death for your investment program.

QUICK REVIEW

1. Having enough insurance to cover any loans on your property will be required by lenders.
2. In addition, rent loss coverage, natural disaster coverage, and coverage on a swimming pool are all products a landlord may need to consider.
3. A blanket liability policy is also a good idea.

Ideas are a dime a dozen. People who put them into action are priceless.

PUTTING IT ALL TOGETHER AND CREATING YOUR GAME PLAN

PUTTING IT ALL TOGETHER AND CREATING A GAME PLAN

We have covered a lot of material. Now let's put it all together and get started at creating your "game plan." Let's start with the basics and work our way up your investment ladder.

1. Get your finances in order. Pay down credit cards and other monthly obligations. Start saving money for deposits, closing costs and down payment.

2. Get a current copy of your credit report with FICO scores (not the credit scores provided by the credit bureaus). FICO scores are a grading system for credit reports that was developed by Fair Isaac Corp. At this time, the mortgage industry exclusively uses FICO Scores. You can get your FICO scores at **www.myFICO.com**.

3. Start cleaning up your credit (if necessary). Remember it takes months to repair credit reports. Remove any inaccurate information or accounts that are not yours and verify all account balances and monthly payments. If you need help contact a mortgage broker or banker.

4. If you have been renting, have you made all of your rent payments on time for the last 12 months? This is very important. Have you had stability in your employment or other sources of income for the last two years? If the answer is "no," to either of these two questions, you may not be financially ready for home ownership.

5. Build a relationship with a REALTOR®, a loan officer and a property manager. Let them guide you in your preparation. If you are an investor or plan to become one, make sure that your team has experience with investment properties. You need to work with people that will be part of "your team" on whom you can depend now and in the future.

6. If your credit and finances are in order, it may be time to start previewing properties. Take your time and do it right. Do not rush the process. Remember this is a major business decision.

7. Refer back to the following list of "Eight Pillars" and the list of "Insights." Let them provide you with guidance through the buying process. You may want to make your REALTOR® and/or loan officer aware of this material so they can understand what you are trying to accomplish and why.

8. Be aware that team members work for each other. If you expect your team to be there when you need their assistance and guidance, you need to provide them with your current and future business. They cannot afford to provide you with their time, knowledge and experience if they cannot count on receiving your current and future business. REALTORS® and loan officers do not receive monthly salaries; they are only compensated if a transaction is completed.

I sincerely hope that this material has given you enough information to make you comfortable with whatever plans you may have for real estate investing. Knowledge is powerful, if it is put to use. Now is the time for you to utilize it for you and your family's financial future. *Make your plans and work your plan. Please get started now.*

If you have any questions about any of this material feel free to send me an e-mail, and I will respond to your request as soon as possible. I would like to have your feedback on this material or possibly any other ideas that you may have about investing in real estate. If you would like to contact me, I would be glad to hear from you. I can be contacted at **lggarrett@cox.net** or **azmortgageman@cox.net**.

MY PILLARS AND INSIGHTS

My Pillars and Insights for successful Real Estate investing with the goals of minimizing maintenance and management costs, while maximizing long term appreciation and limiting selling costs.

PILLARS

Pillar 1: You should be Excited and Enthusiastic About Investing.

Pillar 2: You Need to be Able to See Long Term Potential in a Property.

Pillar 3: The 20/20/60 Rule; Buy Smart, Manage Well, Sell High.

Pillar 4: To Maximize your Appreciation, Stay Close to Centers of Employment.

Pillar 5: Buy into Growth Areas.

Pillar 6: The Yield Curve is the Best Leading Indicator.

Pillar 7: Location, Location, Location.

Pillar 8: Timing is as Important as Location.

INSIGHTS

Insight 1: Do Not Fight the Fed.

Insight 2: As Interest Rates Go Up, Property Values Decline.

Insight 3: As Interest Rates Go Up, Rents Increase.

COMMON SENSE INVESTING

Insight 4: The Federal Reserve.

Insight 5: The Yield Curve, Better Than a Crystal Ball.

Insight 6: The "Tilt-a Whirl" Ride.

Insight 7: Newer Properties Appreciate Faster.

Insight 8: You Must Have Adequate Reserves.

Insight 9: Two Big Common Mistakes that Investors Make.

Insight 10: If Something Can Go Wrong, It Probably Will.

Insight 11: Fool's Gold.

Insight 12: Real Gold.

Insight 13: Make Money in a Slow Market.

Insight 14: Buy into a Soft Market.

Insight 15: Check Out Recent Comparables Sales and Comparable Rents.

Insight 16: Fools Rush in Where Angels Fear to Tread.

Insight 17: The Magic of the Internet.

Insight 18: Buying a House can be Confusing.

Insight 19: Consumer Debt Versus Investment Debt.

Insight 20: Understand Your Mortgage Options.

Insight 21: There is No Such Thing as a "No Costs Mortgage."

Insight 22: Use an Experienced REALTOR® and Loan Officer.

Insight 23: Your First Real Estate Purchase should be Owner-Occupied.

Insight 24: Real Estate should be a Long-Term Investment.

Insight 25: Hold on for the Long Haul.

Insight 26: The Pros and Cons of Negative Cash Flow.

Insight 27: A Reverse Mortgage can be a Retiree's Financial Salvation.

Insight 28: You are Buying to Sell.

Insight 29: In a Slow Market, Outlying Areas Get Hit the Hardest.

MY PILLARS AND INSIGHTS

Insight 30: Condos are the First to Go Down in Value, Go Down the Farthest, and Stay Down the Longest.

Insight 31: Think About What You Are Buying.

Insight 32: High Demand or High Dollar Areas Will Appreciate.

Insight 33: Schools are Very Important.

Insight 34: Never Confuse Brains with a Bull Market.

Insight 35: How to Calculate the Purchase Price of a "Fixer-up" Property.

Insight 36: Have Several Systems for Buying Property.

Insight 37: How to Make Money in a "No-Growth Economy."

Insight 38: Pricing for a Fast and Profitable Sale

Insight 39: Property Management Can Make or Break You.

Insight 40: Know Your Local & State Government Regulations.

Insight 41: Holding Title – I Do Not Own Anything.

Insight 42: Good Insurance Protects Your Assets.

MORTGAGE AND REAL ESTATE TERMS GLOSSARY

MORTGAGE AND REAL ESTATE TERMS GLOSSARY

Abstract
A historical summary of all the recorded transactions that affect the title to a property.

Acceleration Clause
The clause in a mortgage or trust deed that stipulates the entire debt is due and payable if the borrower defaults under the terms of the contract.

Acceptance
A seller's consent to enter into a contract and be bound by the terms of the offer. In real estate the buyer makes an offer to the seller; if the seller accepts the offer, it becomes a legally binding contract.

Acquisition Costs
Under an FHA loan, acquisition costs are the purchase price or appraised value of the property plus the estimated closing costs.

Adjusted Basis
The adjusted basis is the value used to determine capital gains when the property is sold. It is the original cost of the property plus the value of any capital expenditures for improvements, minus any depreciation taken.

Adjustable Rate Mortgage
A mortgage in which the interest rate changes periodically, according to fluctuations in an index. All "Arms" are tied to an adjustable index.

Adjustment Date

The date the interest rate changes on an ARM.

Adjustment Interval

The time between changes in the interest rates on an ARM loan.

Affordability Analysis

A detailed analysis to determine what price home a purchaser can afford to buy. It takes into account income, liabilities, closing costs and available funds, along with the best type of loan available for the borrower.

Amortization

Literally to "kill off" the outstanding balance of a loan by making equal payments on a regular schedule. The payments are structured so that the borrower pays both interest and principle with equal payment over the life of the loan.

Annual Percentage Rate

The effective rate of interest for a loan on an annual basis. The APR is typically higher than the rate of interest because it includes some closing costs. This is one way to compare two different loans offered by two different companies, but be aware that different companies calculate closing costs differently.

Annuity

A financial instrument purchased so as to secure the right to receive a series of payments regularly, over a period of time, or for life.

Application

The form used to apply for a mortgage loan which contains information about the borrower's income, savings, assets, debts and more.

MORTGAGE AND REAL ESTATE TERMS GLOSSARY

Application Fee

A fee charged by many lenders to the borrower for applying for a loan. Payment of this fee does not guarantee loan approval. Some lenders may apply the costs of the application fee to certain closing costs.

Appraisal

A written determination of a property's current market value based on recent sales of similar properties.

Appraised Value

An opinion of a property's fair market value, based on an appraiser's knowledge, experience, and analysis of the property. The value is based on comparable sales in the immediate area of the subject property.

Appreciation

The increase in value of a property due to changes in market conditions, inflation, and demand for local housing.

Assessment

The placing of a value on property for the purpose of taxation.

Asset

Items of value owned by an individual. Assets that can be quickly converted to cash are considered "liquid assets". These include bank accounts, stocks, bonds, mutual funds, and so on. Other assets include real estate, personal property, and businesses owned by the individual.

Assumable Mortgage

A mortgage that can be assumed by a buyer when a home is sold. Usually the borrower must qualify to assume the loan.

Back-end Ratio

The amount of money that is paid in monthly debts, car payments, student loans, credit cards, and house payment divided by your gross monthly income.

Balloon Mortgage

A mortgage that must be paid off in full before the loan is fully amortized. A loan may be amortized over thirty years but becomes due and payable after ten years.

Bankruptcy

A legal process in which individuals relieve themselves of debts and/or liabilities when they are no longer able to repay the obligations. Borrowers who have undergone bankruptcy usually cannot qualify for "A" paper loans until re-establishing their credit.

Best Faith Estimate

An estimate of the costs for securing a real estate loan that is given to a borrower prior to closing.

Blanket Mortgage

A mortgage secured by the pledging of more than one property.

Bond

An instrument of debt that is sold on the capital markets.

Bond Market

The market for the buying and selling of treasury bills, corporate and government bonds. Lenders follow this market intensely because as the yield of bonds change mortgage rates change in the same direction.

Borrower

A person who receives funds in the form of a loan with the obligation to repay the loan.

MORTGAGE AND REAL ESTATE TERMS GLOSSARY

Broker

An individual in the business of assisting in arranging funding or negotiating contracts for a client, but who does not loan their personal money. Brokers usually charge a fee or receive a commission for their services.

Budget Mortgage

A mortgage that includes a portion for taxes and insurance as well as principal and interest.

Buy down

Allows loans to be made at less-than-market interest rates by paying front-end discounts. The interest rate is "bought down" for a temporary period. In order to acquire this discount, a lump sum is paid and held in an account used to supplement the borrower's monthly payment.

Capital Gains

When a capital asset is sold at a profit, the difference between the amount it sold for and the basis in the property is the capital gains.

Caps

A set percentage amount by which an adjustable rate mortgage may adjust each adjustment period. Adjustable loan caps are usually quoted as two numbers such as 2/6. The first number indicates how much a loan may adjust at each adjustment period while the second number indicates how much a loan may adjust over its lifetime.

Carry back Loans

A loan in which a seller agrees to finance a buyer in order to complete a property sale.

Cash-Out Refinance

A borrower refinances his mortgage at a higher loan amount than his current loan balance so as to pull money out for personal reasons.

Caveat Emptor

A legal term meaning "let the buyer beware." The buyer is buying "in as-is condition" and assumes all responsibility for the condition of the asset.

Certificate of Deposit

A time deposit held in a bank which pays a certain amount of interest to the depositor.

Certificate of Eligibility

A veteran's evidence of entitlement for a VA-guaranteed loan.

Certificate of Reasonable Value

An appraisal that has been performed on a property that is being financed with a VA loan. After the appraisal the Veterans Administration issues a CRV.

Chain of Title

An analysis of the transfers of title to a parcel of property over the years.

Clear Title

A title that is free of liens or legal clouds as to ownership of the property.

Closing

This has different meanings in different states. In some states a real estate transaction is not considered "closed" until the documents are recorded at the local recorder's office. In others, the "closing" is a meeting where all of the documents are signed and money changes hands.

Closing Costs

Closing costs are separated into what are called "non-recurring closing costs" and "pre-paid items". Non-recurring closing costs are any items which are paid just once as a result of financing the purchase of a property. "Pre-paids" are items which recur over time, such as property taxes and insurance. A lender is required to estimate the amount of non-recurring closing costs and pre-paid items on the Good Faith Estimate which must be issued within three days of receiving a loan application.

Co-borrower
An individual who is both obligated on the loan and is listed on the title to the property.

Collateral
The property in a residential loan is the security given as a pledge for the repayment of a loan. If the borrower does not perform according to the terms of the loan he may lose the property to a foreclosure.

Collection
When a borrower falls behind in his payments on an obligation as part of the collection effort the loan goes into "collection."

Commission
Most salespeople earn commissions for the work they perform for their clients or employers. The commissions are paid out of the charges paid for by the sellers or buyers in the purchase transaction.

Commitment
A written letter of agreement detailing the terms and conditions by which the lender will lend, and the borrower will borrow funds to finance a purchase.

Comparable Sales
Recent sales of similar properties in nearby areas used to help determine the market value of property.

Condominium
A type of ownership in which all of the owners own the property, common area, and buildings with the exception of the interior of the unit in for which they hold title.

Conforming Loan
A loan amount that conforms to Fannie Mae and Freddie Mac guidelines.

Construction Loan
A short term loan for funding the construction costs of building a structure.

Contingency
A condition which must be met before a contract is legally binding. For instance, a buyer may make an offer subject to approving a property inspection or obtaining a termite clearance.

Contract
A written or oral agreement to do or not to do a certain thing.

Conventional Mortgage
A mortgage loan that is not guaranteed by a government agency.

Credit Loan
A loan that is issued only on the financial strength of a borrower without regard for collateral.

Credit Rating
A credit rating is a measure of a borrower's credit worthiness or risk level. Credit ratings are based on the borrower's payment history, foreclosures, bankruptcies and charge-offs.

Credit Report
A report about the credit standing of a prospective borrower is used to determine creditworthiness.

Creditor
A person or organization to whom money is owed.

Credit Repository
A company that gathers, records, updates and stores financial and public records information about payment records of individuals.

MORTGAGE AND REAL ESTATE TERMS GLOSSARY

Debt

An amount of money owed to another.

Deed

A legal document conveying title to a property.

Deed of Trust

Synonymous with a mortgage. A deed of trust or mortgage is a legal document that secures a debt with real estate.

Default

The failure to make timely payments on a loan.

Delinquency

Failure to make timely payments on a debt.

Depreciation

The decline of the value of improvements built on real estate. Depreciation is also an accounting term used to expense the reduced value of improvements and used to reduce the borrower's taxable income.

Discount Points

Difference in the face amount of a note or mortgage and the price at which the instrument is sold in the secondary market. Fees paid to a lender to reduce the interest rate.

Down Payment

Money paid down by the borrower from his own funds and does not finance with a mortgage.

Earnest Money Deposit

A cash deposit made by a buyer to indicate that he is serious about purchasing a property.

Economic Indicators

A series of statistical figures used by economists to predict future economic activity such as, the consumer price index or gross domestic products

Effective Age

An appraiser's estimate of the physical condition of a building. The actual age may be shorter or longer than its effective age.

Encroachment

An improvement that intrudes illegally on another's property

Encumbrance

Any lien against a property or any restriction on its use.

Equity

The difference between the current market value of a property and the principal balance of all outstanding liens.

Escrow

A third party agent who receives, holds, and/or disburses certain funds or documents upon the performance of certain conditions.

Escrow Account

An account that a borrower holds with a lender once a transaction is closed. This requires the borrower to pay additional monies beyond the interest and principle payments. Typically the additional funds would cover property taxes and homeowners insurance.

Escrow Analysis

An analysis by the lender each year to show that the correct amount of money is collected and distributed to cover the various expenses.

Escrow Fee

A charge for the preparation and transmission of all home purchase-related documents and funds.

Estate

This is the sum total of all real and personal property owned by an individual.

Eviction

The legal removal of occupants of real estate who are not meeting the terms of their lease or rental agreement.

Fair Market Value

The highest price that a buyer would be willing to pay, but not compelled to buy, and the lowest price a seller, willing but not compelled to sell, would accept.

Fannie Mae

The Federal National Mortgage Association is a congressionally chartered, shareholder-owned company. This organization is the largest buyer of home mortgage loans.

Federal Housing Administration

An agency under the U.S. Department of Housing and Urban Development which insures loans made by approved lenders to qualified borrowers, in accordance to its regulations and guidelines.

Federal Reserve Bank

The nation's central banking system which was created to stimulate economic growth, fight inflation, increase employment, stabilize the economy and increase national security.

Fee Simple

The best title that one can obtain: unqualified and conveys the highest bundle of rights.

FHA Mortgage
A government backed loan that is insured by FHA. Along with a VA loan, these are often referred to as government backed loans.

FICO
Credit scores calculated by Fair Isaac Company are often referred to as FICO scores.

Finance Charge
The total costs involved in obtaining a loan.

Firm Commitment
A lender's written agreement to provide a loan to a specific borrower at specific terms and conditions.

First Mortgage
A mortgage which has priority over any other mortgage. It is usually determined by the recording dates of the various mortgages.

Fixed Rate Mortgage
A mortgage where the interest rate does not change over the life of the mortgage.

Fixture
Personal property that becomes real property when permanently attached to the real property.

Flat Yield Curve
A unique situation in which the interest rate yield on short term bills and long term bonds are virtually the same.

Flood Insurance
Insurance that compensates for physical damage caused by flooding. It is required on all properties located in federally designated flood areas.

Mortgage and Real Estate Terms Glossary

Front-end Ratio

Monthly housing expense for principal, interest, taxes and insurance divided by monthly gross income.

Foreclosure

A legal procedure in which real estate is sold by the lender to pay a defaulting borrower's debts.

Good Faith Estimate

An estimate of charges which a borrower is likely to pay in connection with obtaining a new loan.

Government National Mortgage Association

A government-owned corporation within the U.S. Department of Housing and Urban Development. GNMA provides the same services Fannie Mae and Freddie Mac in providing funds to lenders for making home loans. Ginnie Mae provides funds for FHA and VA loans.

Gross Monthly Income

The total monthly income of a borrower before any deductions for taxes and payroll deductions. Used in calculations to determine how much a borrower can afford for a monthly payment.

Hazard Insurance

An insurance policy that protects the insured against loss for fire, vandalism, wind damages, and other natural causes but not flood damage.

Home Equity Conversion Mortgage

Commonly referred to as a reverse mortgage. This mortgage provides income to the borrower, and is designed for elderly homeowners who need income and do not want to sell their residence. The borrower must be 62 years old or older. No income is required to qualify and the loan is not based on the borrower's credit. The loan is based on the amount of equity in the property and the age of the youngest borrower.

Home Equity Line of Credit

Typically, a second mortgage that allows borrowers to obtain cash drawn against a line of credit up to an approved loan amount.

Home Inspection

A thorough inspection by a licensed home inspector regarding the structural and mechanical condition of a property.

Homeowner's Insurance

An insurance policy that combines personal liability insurance and hazard insurance for a home and its contents.

Homeowner's Warranty

An insurance policy typically purchased by a new homeowner to insure the appliances, heating and cooling, electrical and plumping fixtures for a certain time period.

Housing Ratio

The ratio of the monthly housing payment to total gross income, also called front–end ratio.

HUD

Department of Housing and Urban Development that regulates Fannie Mae and Ginnie Mae.

Impound Account

That portion of the borrower's monthly payment held by the lender or servicer to pay for taxes, hazard insurance, mortgage insurance and other items as they become due and payable.

Income Property

Real Estate which generates rental income.

Index
> A published index which lenders use to adjust the interest rate on adjustable mortgages. There are many various indices which lenders use as a basis for their adjustable rate mortgages.

Inflation
> An increase in the general level of prices which is a decrease in the purchasing power of a country's money.

Insight
> An understanding of relationships that sheds light on or helps solve a problem. An understanding of the motivational forces behind one's actions, thoughts or behavior.

Interest
> Monies paid to borrow money; interest rates are usually stated as a percentage rate of the amount of money borrowed.

Inverted Yield Curve
> The interest rate yields on long term bonds are less than the interest rate yield on short term bills. This situation usually signals that the economy is headed into a recessionary situation.

Jumbo Loan
> A loan amount that exceeds Fannie Mae's and Freddie Mac's conforming loan limits.

Lease
> A written agreement between the property owner and a tenant that stipulates the payment and conditions under which the tenant may posses the real estate for a specified time period.

Lease Option
> An alternative financing option that allows home buyers to lease a home with an option to buy.

Lender

A term which can refer to the institution making the loan or to the individual representing the firm.

Liabilities

A person's financial obligations which may include both long-term debts as well as short-term debts.

Liability Insurance

Insurance coverage that offers protection against claims alleging that a property owner's negligence or inappropriate action resulted in bodily injury or property damage to another party.

Lien

A legal claim against a property that must be paid when selling the property to clear title to the property.

Life Cap

A limit on the amount that the interest rate can be raised over the life of an adjustable rate loan.

Leading Indicator

A measurable economic factor that changes before the economy starts to follow a particular pattern or trend. Leading indicators are used to predict changes in the economy before the changes occur. Bond yields are typically a good leading indicator of the market because traders anticipate trends in the economy.

Loan to Value

The percentage relationship between the amount of the loan and the appraised value of the property.

Margin

The margin is a fixed number added to a variable index to compute the interest rate on an adjustable mortgage.

Median Sales Price

To calculate the median sales price, find the price for which one half of the assets sold for more and one half sold for less. The price in the middle of the range is the median.

Merged Credit Report

A credit report which includes the credit information from two, or more, credit agencies combined into a single credit report.

Monthly Housing Expense

The total of monthly principal, interest, taxes, and insurance paid by a borrower. This figure is divided by the gross income to calculate the front-end ratio.

Mortgage

A legal document that pledges property to a creditor for the repayment of a loan.

Mortgage Banker

A mortgage banker originates and funds the loans with his company's money.

Mortgage Broker

A broker originates a loan which is funded by a third party, usually a bank or mortgage banker.

Negative Amortization

An increase in the principal balance which occurs when the monthly payment does not cover all of the interest costs.

No Cash-Out Refinancing

This type of loan is referred to as a "rate and term refinance." The original loan balance plus any costs incurred in obtaining the new loan are added together to determine the new loan balance.

No-Cost Loan

The lender covers all or part of the costs of obtaining a new loan. The lender charges an interest rate that is higher than the market rate to cover the costs of the loan.

No-Doc Loan

A loan requiring very little documentation, the down payment is usually 25% and the interest rate is usually higher than a full doc loan.

Normal Yield Curve

A normal yield curve shows short term bill yields lower than long term bond yields. The longer the bond is written for the higher the yield.

Note

A legal document that obligates a borrower to repay a mortgage at specified terms and conditions.

Note Rate

The interest rate stated on a note.

Origination Fee

A fee charged by the lender to process a new loan. Typically, the lender will charge a point, which is 1% of the loan amount. Discount points may also be charged by the lender, a discount point should lower the interest rate below the current market rates at the time of closing.

Owner Financing

A transaction in which the seller carries all or part of the financing to expedite the sale.

Periodic Payment Cap

A limit on the amount that a payment can change during any one adjustment period.

MORTGAGE AND REAL ESTATE TERMS GLOSSARY

Periodic Rate Cap

A limit on the amount that the interest rate can change during any one adjustment period.

Personal Property

Any property that is not real estate.

Pillar

A prominent support. A structure or part that provides support and resembles a column or pillar and this book's definition.

PITI

Abbreviation for principal, interest, taxes, and insurance.

Point

One percent of the loan amount.

Prepayment Penalty

A fee that is charged by the lender if the borrower pays off a loan before a specified time period.

Prime Rate

The interest rate that lenders charge their best customers.

Principal

The amount originally borrowed or the amount remaining unpaid.

Private Mortgage Insurance

Insurance provided by a private insurance company that insures the lender against loss on the amount of the loan that exceeds 80% of the loan to value.

Promissory Note

A legal contract in which the borrower promises to pay a specified amount per certain terms and conditions.

Purchase Agreement

A written contract signed by the buyer and seller stating the terms and conditions of the sale.

Qualifying Ratios

Two ratios are calculated in determining for how much a loan a borrower can qualify. The front-end ratio is the monthly housing payment divided by the borrower's monthly gross income. This ratio should not exceed 28% of the borrower's gross monthly income. The second ratio is called the back-end ratio. It is calculated by dividing all of the borrower's monthly debt payments including the new house payment by their monthly gross income. This ratio should not exceed about 40% of their gross monthly income.

Quitclaim Deed

A deed which transfers whatever interest or title a grantor may have in a property, if any.

Rate Lock

A written commitment by a lender to a borrower guaranteeing a specified interest rate for a specified time period.

Real Estate

A portion of the earth's surface extending downward to the center of the earth and upward into space.

Real Estate Agent

A person licensed by the state to negotiate and transact the sale of real estate.

REALTOR®

A real estate agent or broker who holds active membership in a local real estate board that is affiliated with the National Association of REALTORS®.

Recorder

A public official who keeps records of real estate transactions and makes them part of the public records.

Recording
The noting of a properly executed legal document, thereby making it a part of the public record.

Redlining
The practice of refusing to lend or insure in certain neighborhoods.

Refinance Transaction
The process of paying off one loan with the proceeds from a new loan.

Rent Loss Insurance
Insurance that protects a landlord against lost rent due to fire or other casualty in which the premises is unavailable for occupancy.

Revolving Debt
Usually debts associated with the use of credit cards.

Right of First Refusal
A provision in an agreement that requires the owner of a property to give another party the first opportunity to purchase the property before offering it to another party.

Second Mortgage
A mortgage that has a lien position after another recorded mortgage.

Secondary Market
The buying and selling of existing mortgages.

Secured Loan
A loan that is secured by collateral.

Security
The property that is pledged as collateral for a loan.

Seller Carry-Back

An agreement in which a seller of a property provides financing for the buyer.

Servicing

The collection of mortgage payments from the borrower and the disbursement of the funds to the appropriate parties.

Sub Prime Loan

High-risk loans with interest rates normally much higher than normal conforming rates. The borrowers have less than perfect credit, and may have high outstanding debts or unproven income.

Subordinate Financing

Any lien or mortgage that has a lower priority than a first lien.

Survey

A drawing showing the legal boundaries of a property, improvements, easements and other physical features.

Tax Lien

A lien against real estate for unpaid property taxes.

Title

A legal document showing ownership of a property.

Title Company

A company that specializes in examining and insuring titles to real estate.

Title Insurance

Insurance that protects a lender or the buyer against loss from disputes over ownership of property.

Title Search
A search of the public records to ensure that the seller is the legal owner of the property and that there are no liens against the property.

Transfer of Ownership
The process by which property ownership of property changes hands.

Truth-in-Lending
A provision in which a lender is required to reveal the actual costs of borrowing.

Underwriting
The decision whether to make a loan to a borrower based on income, credit, stability of employment, assets, etc.

Walk-Through Inspection
A final walk-through immediately before the close of escrow to verify that no changes have taken place and that there is no new damage to the property.

VA Loan
A government backed mortgage loan guaranteed by the US Veterans Administration.

Vested
Having the right to use a portion of a fund such as an individual retirement fund.

Veterans Administration (VA)
An agency of the federal government that guarantees residential mortgages to eligible veterans of the military service.

Yield Curve

A line that plots the interest rates, at a set point in time, of bonds having equal credit value but differing maturity dates. The most frequently reported yield curve compares the three month bill, two year, five year, ten year and thirty year bonds. This yield curve is used as a benchmark for other debt in the markets. The curve is also used to predict economic output and growth. The shape of the yield curve is closely scrutinized as it helps to predict future interest rate changes and economic activity. This leading economic indicator has been correct over 80% of the time for the last forty-five years.

Zoning

The right of a community by its policing powers to dictate the use of property within its boundaries.

www.ingramcontent.com/pod-product-compliance
Ingram Content Group UK Ltd.
Pitfield, Milton Keynes, MK11 3LW, UK
UKHW051256180426
11947UKWH00020B/1736